WANTING TO BELIEVE

FAITH, FAMILY, AND FINDING AN EXCEPTIONAL LIFE

RYAN DOBSON

WANTING TO BELIEVE

FAITH, FAMILY, AND FINDING AN EXCEPTIONAL LIFE

B&H
PUBLISHING GROUP

NASHVILLE, TENNESSEE

978-1-4336-8252-0

Published by B&H Publishing Group
Nashville, Tennessee

Dewey Decimal Classification: 248.84
Subject Heading: FAITH \ FAMILY \ CHRISTIAN LIFE

Ryan Dobson is represented by the literary agency
of Wolgemuth & Associates, Inc.

Unless otherwise noted, Scripture quotations are from the Holy
Bible, New International Version, copyright © 1973, 1978, 1984
by International Bible Society. Also used: the New American
Standard Bible (NASB) © the Lockman Foundation, 1960, 1962,
1963, 1968, 1971, 1972, 1973, 1975, 1977, used by permission.

1 2 3 4 5 6 7 • 18 17 16 15 14

God is at home; it is we who have gone for a walk.

—MEISTER ECKHART

contents

introduction

why this, why now

I do believe; help my unbelief.

—Mark 9:24 NASB

A father once had a son. As most fathers do, this father absolutely treasured his son, but there were issues with the son—big issues, other-worldly issues, issues the father felt powerless to resolve. The son actually was "possessed with a spirit which makes him mute," the father would explain, "and whenever it seizes him, it slams him to the ground and he foams at the mouth, and grinds his teeth and stiffens out" (Mark 9:17–18 NASB).

The father called on Jesus to help; he asked the Healer if He would please heal his son.

Jesus told the father to bring to Him the son, and the father quickly did. "If You can do anything," the father pleaded, "take pity on us and help us!" to which Jesus said, "'If You can?' All things are possible to him who believes."

The father looked at Jesus and said, "I do believe; help my unbelief" (vv. 22–24 NASB).

Jesus then healed the son, rebuking the unclean spirit to depart from him and restoring the boy to full and complete health. But the healing of the son has always struck me as less important here than the father's paradoxical faith.

I do believe; help my unbelief.

I can relate to those words. If I had to sum up my faith journey in six words, in fact, I would pick those words. I do believe. Help my unbelief.

Belief tends to go like that.

I spend a good amount of my time these days traveling around the country, speaking to audiences about God. I talk about the character of God, the presence and power of God, and what following God fully requires. In short, I hand over *truth* and invite everyone listening to reach out and take it in. I know from personal experience it's a long and difficult reach. We want to believe truth, to grasp it and make it our own, but something in us revolts. Something in us just can't take truth.

I do believe; help my unbelief.

We so desperately want to believe.

After every talk I give, I stand at the front of the stage and invite people to come over and talk with me. For nearly fifteen years I've been doing this, and one theme has characterized those one-on-one chats more than any other theme: *wanting to believe.*

"I want to believe that what you're saying is true," they'll explain, "but given my background, it's such a stretch."

Yes. To reach out and grasp truth and take it in—it's a long and difficult reach.

"I completely understand," I always say in response. "My advice to you? Choose to believe."

They've never thought of it that way, but it remains true. Belief is always a choice.

I've made some spectacularly bad choices throughout my life—many of which appear in the pages to come—but if there is one reason I kept coming back to truth, kept returning to add another layer to the foundation of faith on which my life has been built, that reason is my dad.

Dr. James C. Dobson has spent the entirety of his professional life telling the truth, and those truths have formed not only the successful structure by which I live my life, but also, more immediately, the chapters of this book. My hope in putting a few of those lessons down here, in sentences and paragraphs and pages, is that for the first time or for the millionth, you'll encounter truth in all its startling beauty, and you'll make the choice to believe it really is true.

1

the Lord will lead

*Being a Christian is less about cautiously avoiding sin than
about courageously and actively doing God's will.*
—DIETRICH BONHOEFFER

ost Christians I know don't really want to follow Christ. We
think we do. We say we do. We even tend to *believe* that we
do. But mostly, we don't. We'd rather follow ourselves—our
own schemes and plans and whims and ways. Brilliant author Eric
Metaxes puts it this way: "People say they want to follow God, but
too often they do only if it's in an advisory role."

As I say, this is most Christians.

My parents have never been "most Christians."

Many years ago, a couple I know had a baby girl. This was a joyous experience because they had prayed and prayed for a baby, and now at last a baby was theirs. As days and weeks and months went by, that little baby began to giggle and gurgle and talk and walk, and with each step of development the couple was bubbled over with excitement and contentment and joy—all because of this precious little girl. They would go on walks with her and sing songs with her and get down on the carpeted floor of the living room to play tea party and the silly, childish games she wanted to play, all because they adored her, because they loved being parents that much.

A couple of years passed, and the couple still felt enamored of this little girl. To each other they said, "This is amazing. We should do this again. *We should have another child.*" And so the plan was set; they would get pregnant again. But life doesn't always go according to plan.

Soon it was discovered that there were "problems" and that the wife had several "issues" and that conceiving again would be a "challenge" for this man and wife. With these grim pronouncements from medical professionals accompanying them, they went home and cried and regrouped.

"We want another baby," they whispered between them, "but we want God's will more." They decided to make a deal. Every night before they went to sleep, they would kneel beside their bed and pray. They would ask God for His insight, and they would remind Him of their heartfelt desire. And with that, they set off on this journey, the journey of letting God be God.

They prayed for an entire year this way, every night, three hundred and sixty-five nights in a row. Night after night they knelt and they prayed. And at the end of that year . . . nothing.

Nothing happened.

No answer to prayer.

No insight from God.

No sibling for their adorable little girl.

And so they signed on for another year. Every night for another full year, they prayed and prayed and prayed. The end of that second year came, and . . . nothing. Again. No answer. No insight. No child.

God wasn't saying, "Wait," mind you. Nor was He saying, "No." What He was saying was exactly *nothing*, and nothing is hard to take.

They agreed to pray a third year, and then, after that, a fourth. *Four years* of praying every single night, for God to lead them in His perfect will. But still: no answer, no insight, no child. I can't believe they had the strength to go on. I myself don't become impatient after four years in prayer; I become impatient after four *minutes* in prayer.

But for four years and then some they prayed and they prayed, and they trusted that God would lead.

Unbeknownst to this couple, there was another couple that was in high school at the time, a couple that God would use in answering their prayer.

These high schoolers would do the things all young lovers do. They would go out to dinner and go to the movies and talk all night on the phone. This was in the day when phones had cords, and I like to imagine the girl sneaking into a coat closet in her parents' home and hanging on every word the boy said. They probably ended their calls the same way we all did back then, where he says, "Okay, you hang up," to which she says, "No, you hang up."

"No, you."

"No, *you*."

"Okay. On the count of three we both hang up, ready? One . . . two . . ."

They were truly in love—they both would swear it—but eventually the girl realized this wasn't the boy she wanted to marry someday, and so they broke up and went separate ways. Soon after their split, the girl discovered she was pregnant. Pregnant and alone and seventeen years old. What was she to do?

She scoured her mind for options: keep the baby, abort the baby, give the baby up for adoption—none of these seemed desirable, but she knew she had to do something soon. She had kept the information from her parents, fearful that they'd be angry or, worse, disappointed. But the time came when she had to come clean. She needed their help and she knew it; she'd just have to tell them the truth.

After the initial shock of the admission wore off, the girl and her family began praying for solutions. They asked people of prayer at their church for help, which is when they were pointed to the services of a pregnancy resource center. They called a counselor there, they made an appointment to meet, and they began making arrangements for the baby that soon would be born.

There's a verse in Romans 8 that we rattle off with such frequency we often forget how utterly profound it is. Verse 28 says, "And we know that in all things God works for the good of those who love him, who have been called according to his purpose." We tend to think it's our magnificent machinations that cause good things to happen in life, but this verse begs to differ; in fact, it's God at work. In this case, the "good" that came about was that the Lord took one faithful couple's inability to conceive again and a young and rather rebellious couple's angst-ridden mistake, and on August 31, 1970, James and Shirley Dobson brought me home from an adoption agency. I was the tender age of six weeks old.

Their prayers had been working miracles, though they couldn't see it at the time. God was leading, and they were following, and *all* our lives were worked for good as a result.

When I was six years old, my dad made the shift from clinical practice to ministry, and I imagine everyone around him thought he'd gone nuts. Here he was, working at the Children's Hospital Los Angeles, a prestigious psychologist who had great benefits, financial security, and burgeoning notoriety, and yet he up and quit. What's more, he quit to go do *radio*—in the field of psychotherapy no less, a relative unknown.

I imagine that for my mom, this move was terrifying. She had two kids to think about, and the security she'd come to rely on was being haphazardly given up. Or that's how she probably saw it, anyway. "You're going to leave your successful practice and just *hope something happens* on the ministry front?"—this and scores of other questions aimed at her well-meaning husband must have flooded her brain at the time.

And yet "quit and hope something happens" is precisely what my dad did. This, for the record, is how Focus on the Family got its start. It started on a wing and a prayer.

My dad's first radio-ministry office was a modest, two-room situation with a part-time secretary and nature-scene wallpaper in drab hues of chestnut and avocado on every wall. This was 1976, and decorating was a challenge: how do you hang *anything* on a busy grove of trees? The office was brash and small and seemingly lacking in both potential and personality; what on earth had my dad done?

According to him back then and still today, he'd simply "followed God."

Within ten years, my father had seven of the top ten best-selling Christian books, he had upward of five hundred employees, and he was convinced he'd made the right move. Within the next ten years, his staff would multiply to fifteen hundred, with more than seven hundred volunteers in addition to that, and annual revenues would crest at $140 million. By all measures, he was deemed a success.

But *still*, he'd demur when approached.

"This was never my intention," he'd say. "I never asked for the mega-organization. I just wanted to go where God was leading. I wanted to walk by faith."

I think about those years when my dad and mom prayed at their bedside for another child, and I see so clearly how God was grooming them, to become necessary people of prayer. The stuff God wanted to accomplish through my parents wouldn't happen any other way.

The first *Focus on the Family* broadcasts were thirty minutes in length and were aired once weekly, an approach that totally flopped. Once a week was something listeners couldn't seem to grasp—too often they'd forget when the program was on . . . it just wasn't part of their routine. The booking service that had helped my dad get his start in radio said they could make a daily show happen for him; but it wouldn't be cheap, they warned, and the money would be due up front.

For all the professional success my dad had enjoyed to that point, thirty grand was a sum he didn't have ready to burn. He talked with my mom one day and they agreed to begin praying right then, which is when my godfather happened to stop by. Uncle Jim inadvertently interrupted the prayer session, innocently asking what my folks were up to. "We're praying for thirty thousand dollars," my dad said plainly, "to move us from a weekly to a daily show."

Uncle Jim joined hands with my parents, and the three of them then pounded on the doors of heaven, trusting and believing that if my dad's ministry was to flourish, it would only be because God came through.

The next day, the check came, for exactly thirty grand. It was a close family friend who wrote it. God provides.

Certainly all of life wasn't a cake walk for my dad; God is not a slot machine, and prayers don't come with guarantees. But over the years he noticed an interesting dynamic: when he charted his own course he got off-track, but when he deferred to God's ways he thrived. It was because of this realization that my dad developed a certain disdain for long-term planning. Still today, if you ask Dr. James Dobson about his five-year plan or his ten-year plan, you'll see steam shoot from his ears and nose, just before he eases his way out of the room. The question makes him nuts, mostly because the answer is so obvious to him: the long-term plan for a follower of Christ is simply *to follow Christ*. In my dad's words, "It's worked pretty well so far."

Tough to refute that point.

When I was in my mid-twenties, I faced something of a quarter-life crisis, and it had to do with my faith. I called myself a Christian, but I wasn't really following Christ—at least, not in the same manner I observed in my father. I saw a certain intimacy there, between my dad and God, an intimacy I didn't know. And it wasn't just my dad; I began noticing many of my dad's friends—men such as Joe White, Dave Noebel, Josh McDowell, and the late Chuck Colson—they enjoyed that intimacy too. The question that vexed me for several years straight was, "Can *everyone* experience intimacy with Christ, or is it reserved for a special few?"

From age twenty-five to age thirty-two, I wrestled with this question, and after that long, seven-year stretch, an answer finally emerged. On the heels of a difficult marriage and a bitter divorce and hitting rock bottom emotionally, spiritually, and all the rest, I discovered that yes, I could know intimacy with God on par with the spiritual giants I knew firsthand, but that intimacy would cost me everything. There would be a *terribly* stiff price to pay.

I wrote the following words upon making this revelation, words I believe deeply still today:

> Action sports guys like to say that unless your sport could get you killed, it isn't really a sport. It's just a game.
>
> I'd say that's pretty true about life too. If it isn't high-end dangerous, if it isn't risky, if it isn't scary, then it's not really living. It's just a game.

Deep down, we all know this is true. You and I were born for excitement and adventure. Ultimately we can be satisfied with nothing less than the adrenaline-filled life. Anything less leaves us bored. And when we're bored, we're boring.

Even to God.

Jesus once said He'd rather we be cold or hot than lukewarm. Lukewarm means just air-temperature. You're un-hot, you're un-cold. You're simply the same temperature as your environment. Your atmosphere controls you. Your personal spiritual thermostat is disengaged or out of order, so you generate no heat of your own. You're just a slave to your surroundings. You let your background blend you in. You just go with the flow.

When you're like that, Jesus said He feels like vomiting you right out of His mouth.[1]

This, I think, is precisely why so many of us Christ followers want to follow Christ and say we follow Christ and believe we are *of course* following Christ, even as we don't, in fact, follow Him—because to really, truly follow is to really, truly let Him lead. If we will follow, the Lord will lead—that's as complicated as this stuff gets. And yet while it may seem easy on the surface, it's a whole lot harder than it sounds. Because where He leads us to is never a place of lukewarm safety. His leadership *always* leads us to situations and experiences requiring courage, perseverance, and faith.

For the past decade and a half I have made my living with words. I deliver talks, I help host radio programs, and I write about my thoughts on life. I am fully confident this is God's plan

for me, and honestly, I couldn't love anything more. To say I am
obsessed with speaking and writing would be understatement. I
study the craft, I talk with other speakers and writers about the
craft, and if I'm not thinking about my family or skateboarding or
food, I guarantee I'm thinking about how to get better at what I
do. And yet this profession that I am so passionate about, the one
that brings me income and challenge and deep joy, is the very *last*
thing I thought I'd be doing with my life.

In my early twenties I knew I was destined to be president
of the United States, and so I mapped out my life accordingly. I
would graduate from college, I would start local with positions
on school boards and city councils, I would land a seat in state
government—either in Colorado or California—and then by age
fifty-five, I'd make my national bid.

Just prior to this grand scheme being rolled out, I was sitting with my buddy Matt in the Eagle's Nest snack bar at Biola
University in La Mirada, California, where we both attended
school, when Jerry Huson, the baseball coach, approached. To me,
he said, "Excuse me, but are you Ryan Dobson?"

After confirming that he had the right guy, he explained that
he led a camp for junior-high kids each winter and wondered if I
would consider being a speaker that year. Before I could dish up
my unequivocal, "No, no, no. No, I *absolutely* don't want to do
that," he went on. "We'd need a worship leader to open for you,"
he said, "and I know your friend Matt here can sing and play.
What do you say? You both want to give it a go?"

I felt Matt kick me under the table—code for, "Please say yes,
Ryan. I need a gig worse than you know."

My eyes were still fixed on the winter-camp guy, and the expression on my face must have been one of incredulity. I mean, here I was, the future president of the United States, and he wanted me to give up a full weekend of my precious time to come hang out with pimply, pubescent kids? Was he kidding?

A couple of months later, I was standing in front of one hundred pimply, pubescent kids, preaching my ever-loving heart out. And you know what? I loved every minute of it.

It turns out I was destined not to run the largest Superpower in the world, but rather to minister to it. I didn't know this at the time, of course, but someone whose opinion I've always esteemed did. That person is my dad. And when I called him on the heels of receiving that invitation in the Eagle's Nest that day, he said, "Ryan, I think you ought to do this. You would be *fantastic* in a role like that."

My dad knew that I had been in debate and speech competitions my entire life, and that I'd loved every single one. He knew I'd been entered in numerous poetry competitions as early as the second grade, and that I was fascinated by the power of words. He knew that when I was five years old, I had recited Psalm 100 to a room full of three hundred women, and that when I'd taken the stage, I'd scampered over to the podium, climbed atop an apple crate that some stagehands had left sitting there, and boldly pulled the mic down to my level so that even those at the back of the room could hear me talk. He knew I'd been in choir and that I'd acted in various plays and that because I was raised in the context of a family of speakers, I thought it was the most natural thing in the world to stand in front of scores of people and fearlessly say whatever is on your mind. He knew that by age ten I understood the nuances of rhythm and intonation and expression when speaking, and that rather than cowering in the spotlight, I absolutely shone.

He also knew that as a result of attending the Summit, a two-week Christian worldview summer camp when I was seventeen, I had come away awestruck by the character and nature of God, and that a possible use for all that God-centered enthusiasm might be helping others become awestruck too.

"You were made to do this type of thing," he would later tell me, when I went full bore into a speaking career. "This is what you're cut out to do."

I look back on that conversation with my dad about whether I should speak at the junior-high winter camp, and I see divine intervention written all over it. All through Scripture God uses real, live, skin-on-bone types—prophets and priests and apostles as well as unbelievers and even one guy's donkey—to deliver key messages on His behalf. I think God used my dad that day, and thankfully, I listened up. Without dramatizing the situation, my dad's prophetic words set my feet upon the path leading to life that is truly life, which is exactly what God intends.

Referring to His followers in the beloved nation Israel who refused to listen to wise counsel, 2 Chronicles 36:16 (NASB) says, "They continually mocked the messengers of God, despised His words and scoffed at His prophets . . . until there was no remedy." There was no hope for them, because they'd plugged up their ears to the divinely sent messages of God. I think about my initial gut reaction to the speaking invitation—"No, no, no. No, I *absolutely* don't want to do that"—and realize how tragically close I was to burying the best career I'd ever know before it ever got off the ground.

But here's where things get sticky, because despite my loving my career and knowing God has called me to this path and being ridiculously humbled that I get to travel around the world and try to help people match their desire for following Christ with their decision to actually do so, taking my heavenly Father's lead has definitely cost me everything I've ever called my own. My ego, my agenda, my desires, my time, my plans, my preferences, my strength—you name it, I've been asked to lay it down.

Six years ago, I was on the road so much and delivering so many consecutive talks that I all but threw in the towel. My son, Lincoln, was a one-year-old, and I needed to be in Australia for a series of engagements. My wife, Laura, and I packed up our entire family, took our baby on a fourteen-hour flight across the ocean (I don't recommend that), and then proceeded to do thirteen events in four days' time. On top of the rigors of my schedule, we all suffered from major jet lag, which is always a killer for one's emotional state.

We were in Hawaii on vacation, and one afternoon I decided to take a few hours to contemplate ditching the speaking thing and sorting out a brand new life. I happened into a Foodland to get coffee, and while I was waiting in line heard a guy say, "Ryan? Is that you?"

I turned to find Christian Buckley, an old buddy of mine, standing there—inexplicably, since he lived three cities away from me. In California! He explained that he was in town for work but that he had some time to kill. We hung out for an hour or two, during which I explained to him the tension I felt. "I love what

I'm doing," I said, "but I'm doing it too much. And I don't know how to slow the pace."

He gave me some helpful advice on reordering my schedule, but the bigger injection of inspiration he offered centered on reminding me why I loved speaking in the first place. He reconnected me to my passion for talking to people about the things of God, and by the time I left the coffee shop, I felt like I'd been reborn.

The useful reminder I took from that chat was that God's will for us doesn't promise to be easy; it simply promises to be best. Everyone has tough aspects to their calling—for me, it's things like the rigors of travel and the gut-wrenching effects of constant critique. For you, it may be trying to juggle several part-time jobs or trying to care for a special-needs child. For my dad it was forever being labeled by people who misrepresent his heart. We all have a hill to climb, but I tell you, I'd much rather climb the right hill with God's empowerment than to trudge up the wrong one on my own.

My dad would often say, "You can't put limits on God's plan for your life." It was something I didn't fully understand until I started trying to barter with God myself. I'd never have admitted it aloud, but inside, I wanted to negotiate: "I'll follow You, God, as long as the path is smooth and the view is sunny . . ."

"Nope," my dad would remind me. "We don't get to structure things. We just get to say, 'I'm in.'"

As a son who has watched his dad say, "I'm in," thousands of times to his heavenly Father, I can tell you there is no greater goal in parenting than to show your kids how to follow God. The truth about life is that there is so little of it we can control. Sure, we have the illusion of control, but *real* control? That is reserved for God. But He says, "If you follow Me, I will lead you. And My leadership will bring you to life—to life that is *truly* life."

These days, my dad and I will be prepping for a radio broadcast in his office, and the thought will flash across my mind, *I can't believe I get to do this.* I'm part of an amazing ministry and part of an amazing family because this man let God lead. My dad always trusted that God would lead.

finding your exceptional life

1. When have you prayed desperately for something, only to hear silence from heaven in response? Why is divine silence so difficult to take?

2. How would you characterize God's leadership in your life thus far? What significant memories or experiences stand out?

3. What would you hope for your legacy to be regarding going God's way instead of your own? What lessons might friends and family members take from the example you have set?

2

practice what you preach

*You can preach a better sermon with your life
than with your lips.*

—Oliver Goldsmith

y wife, Laura, has only been a Dobson for less than a decade's
time. In so many ways, she married into the madness before
she fully understood the madness that being a Dobson can
be. Our relationship began with a blind date, and just before that
date commenced, she called her sister-in-law, Pam, who was raised
in a Christian home and knew about my dad's ministry and could
offer some perspective on things, and said, "Pam, you've heard of
Dr. James Dobson, right? I'm supposed to go out this weekend
with his son, Ryan."

Pam said, "You're going out with James Dobson's *son*? No way, you don't just *go out* with James Dobson's *son*. There's probably some psychological testing you have to pass first."

In fact, there were no tests. It was just Laura, a million other people in an In-N-Out drive-thru, and me. A very short time after that first date—it could be measured in months—Laura and I were married, and now she was a Dobson, through and through.

Bless her heart.

Soon after we were married, we had our first child, Lincoln. And soon after Lincoln was born, Laura got very involved in MOPS. MOPS is a program for mothers of preschoolers, typically held at churches around this country, and is aimed at helping moms mother well. Laura loves MOPS, not only because they provide stimulating speakers and helpful encouragement for the always rigorous journey of parenthood, but also because there is free childcare and there are free snacks, and sometimes moms just need a break.

When Lincoln was two or three years old, Laura was coming out of one MOPS meeting in particular and had just retrieved Lincoln from that wonderful free childcare, when he decided to have a major meltdown right there in the hallway of the church. All the other MOPS moms were also trying to get their toddlers out of the building and into their cars, and so everyone saw this display.

The meeting, as Laura vividly recalls, was on consequential parenting—that is, how to direct your child's behavior using effective consequences instead of threats or bribes. Laura had nodded in agreement with the speaker the entire time, nonverbally assenting to the ideas that when the parent-child relationship gets sideways, only one of the two people involved has the capacity to choose maturity over madness, dependability over delinquency, and order over sheer chaos. Parents must stay in control of their emotions and of the situation, the thinking went, so they can invite their children to make wise choices or else let natural consequences play out as they may.

There were specific tactics for managing tantrums discussed in that very meeting, as Laura recalls, and now, just after the session—imagine the chances!—my wife was tasked with handling an out-of-control son.

To hear Laura describe it, a holy hush fell over the scene. *What would Laura Dobson do?* There was emphasis on the "Dobson" part of her name as she recounted things for me. In that moment, I felt badly that she had taken my name.

Laura DOBSON was in the same family as JAMES DOBSON, and JAMES DOBSON says dare to discipline your kids. If Laura DOBSON married into the DOBSONS, then surely she'll know what to do. Everyone's attention was rapt, as Lincoln writhed and screamed there on the floor.

This woman is from a family that preaches effective child-rearing, but will she prove she practices what they preach?

Do you practice what you preach?—it's a question that has been tossed my dad's way scores of times a day for nearly forty years running now. Which is actually not surprising, given some of the countercultural things my father has said. In his books and in his talks and during thousands of radio broadcasts, for instance, he has declared that a child should be free to say anything to a parent, as long as it is said with respect and control. And that, contrary to societal input at the time, children actually *crave* boundaries and will thrive only when healthy boundaries are set.

And that transplanted children have the same needs for guidance and discipline as those remaining with their biological parents . . . in other words, unless they've suffered emotional or physical abuse along the way, *spank your adopted kids*. I for one took issue with that idea.

He said that children—and adults too, for that matter—are more than the quality of their nutrition, their genetic heritage, their biochemistry, and the aggregate of parental influences. God has created us all as unique individuals, capable of independent and rational thought that is not attributable to any source, a stance that at the time threw the nature-versus-nurture debate on its head.

He said that kids do better physically, emotionally, and intellectually when their parents care for them at home, as opposed to when they are cared for in a childcare facility. And also that the best way to get children to do what you want them to do is to spend time with them before disciplinary problems occur—having fun together and enjoying mutual laughter and joy, because, according to his research, "when moments of love and closeness happen, kids are not tempted to challenge and test the limits."[2]

He said all these things with passion in his voice and hard, scientific proof behind his words; and while millions of listeners wanted to believe what he was preaching, many of them still needed something more. They needed to know he was actually practicing these principles, in his *own* family and in his *own* home. "You preach a better sermon with your life than with your lips," poet Oliver Goldsmith once said. People had *heard* plenty from my dad; now they wanted to know what he *did*.

For those watching, they would be stunned by what they found: a man who actually lived what he said he believed.

When I was a young child, my dad did something you just don't do, especially when you're an up-and-comer in your career. Just as his work was becoming known and his books were hitting best seller lists and people were seeking his opinion left and right, he *turned down speaking requests*. The year was 1978, and he was trying desperately to make a go of a ministry still in its infancy—according to his publisher, the best thing he could have done was to get "out there," to go on the road, to show up in person and get a loyal following while the getting was good.

My dad said no.

Not long before, my dad had received a letter from his father, admonishing him to keep his priorities straight. "You're experiencing much success early in your career," my grandfather wrote, "but if you succeed in your career and lose your family, you'll regret it." He told my dad to pray for his kids and to let his family hold top spot not only in his heart, but also on his calendar. Which is why when asked to devote himself to life on the road, my dad so quickly and readily said no. "If our loved ones will be treasures to us at the end of our lives," he would later say of the decision, "then why not live like we believe it today?"

It was a radical viewpoint back then and remains a counter-cultural practice today. But it seems to have worked out okay for him: his publisher opted to videotape my dad delivering seven talks on matters pertaining to marriage and the family, which wound up becoming the first film series of Focus on the Family. Total viewership? Eighty million people.

What's more, my dad kept his family intact. He was *present*. He was *engaged*. He enjoyed his kids while we were still kids. He didn't parent perfectly, of course; which parent ever does? But he *practiced* good and noble things and thus has been a good and noble dad.

It's a lesson I take to heart. I'm wired up the same way as my dad—I love my work, I love to challenge myself, and I tend to push and push until I fall down dead-tired. But I know better than to run like this; in fact, I preach a far different theme. I tell everyone who will listen that family is all that really matters, and that kids are only kids once. I tell them to make whatever changes they need to make, in order to prioritize their children, their spouse. I tell them to slow down and be present and pay attention to moments because those moments go by in a flash.

The preaching part is easy; it's the practicing that leaves a little to be desired. And yet here's where the rubber really meets the road. James 1:23–24 says it this way: "Anyone who listens to the word but does not do what it says is like a man who looks at his face in a mirror and, after looking at himself, goes away and immediately forgets what he looks like."

When we hear but don't do, when we preach but don't practice, when we use our lips but not also our lives, we're like that amnesiac guy being described in those verses: we lose touch with the core of who we are.

I'm at my office right now, as I put the finishing touches on this chapter. And yet I desperately want to be home. I've been on the road a lot this month, and I miss my wife and kids. Laura and

I spent twenty minutes on FaceTime last night, her video-calling from our house and me from yet another hotel room, and during that span I got to watch my toddler daughter, Luci, taking her bath. She was splashing water in her own face and cracking herself up, which made Laura and me laugh as well; and while it was sweet, those twenty minutes, it was a far cry from being at home.

I'm tempted to beat myself up over this constant battle I fight—I love my family, and I love my job, and sometimes I feel torn between the two. "There is so much work left to do," my dad often says, "and so little time to do it"—how completely I understand those words; how completely I understand the importance of the work. And yet he and I both know that my grandpa was dead-on: to succeed in our career at the expense of our family is no real success at all.

And so, momentarily, I will shut the lid on this laptop. I will pack up my satchel. And I will climb into my Hulk green, beater of a van and head home. I will sneak in through the front door of our house, take the handful of steps leading up to our family room two at a time, poke my head over the childproof gate at the top of the stairs, and, spotting little Luci, whisper conspiratorially, "Psst! Lu! Come give Daddy kisses!"

She will toddle over to me, all giggles and curls, arms raised in the air, pucker on her tiny lips, and smother my face with wet smooches, and in that moment, my world will be righted, my heart will be full and light. There will be no condemnation for the stuff I missed out on this week, while I was working and traveling and gone. No, there will only be deep gratitude, for this moment, for this girl, for this life.

I'll sweep Luci off her four-inch feet and throw her sack-of-potatoes-style over my shoulder, and together we'll head toward the kitchen, where Laura and Lincoln probably are. There will be laughter and questions and bubbled-over excitement as we swap stories from the day we've just lived. There will be reconnection and renovation and restoration taking place, as we settle back into a rhythm that works. And there will be resolution in my heart of hearts—*these people matter; I will live like they do.*

"This is why I keep practicing," I'll say to myself. "I keep practicing, keep trying, keep refining my schedule, keep maximizing my work hours, keep carving out time to be *here and really here* as much as I possibly can, keep begging God for wisdom and for insight and for grace . . . I keep doing *all* these things—working at it and failing and then working at it better next time—because I believe in what I'm preaching. And I want to practice what I preach." Practice makes perfect, the old saying goes, but in real life, that's just not true. *Practice makes progress* is more often the case, but progress is a decent thing to make.

finding your exceptional life

1. How do you relate to the idea of being pulled in myriad directions and yet wanting to honor your various roles?

2. What does it look like for you to "practice what you preach" in daily life?

3. How do the goals of *perfection* and *progress* differ in your mind and heart? What might an emphasis on progress offer you that striving for perfection never could?

3

money isn't mine

I have done stupid with a lot of zeros on the end of it.
I know what it looks like.

—FINANCIAL-PLANNING GURU DAVE RAMSEY

For an unfortunately brief season of my life, I raked in an obscene amount of money. I had signed on with a speaker's bureau that said they'd send me all over the country to talk about God in front of various audiences—and send me, they did, to the tune of two hundred and fifty days a year. Basically, every other day I'd fly to a different city, I'd be carted around town by a representative from one organization or another, I'd stand on a stage for a couple of hours and speak—one of my *favorite* things to do—and then money would show up in my bank account. A *lot* of money. I was incredulous: I was getting *paid* to do this job?

Who on earth got paid to travel and talk? I felt sure someone was going to show up one day and catch me red-handed living my dream. I just knew the clock was ticking and that at some point the jig would be up.

The money would have been mind-blowing on its own, but for me it was especially mind-blowing because a mere six months previously I had been destitute with a capital D. At thirty years old, I was newly divorced and despairing. I was in debt up to my eyeballs, and I had no job, no savings account, and no prospects for future employment. A ninety-nine-cent fast-food burger was beyond my financial capacity back then. I was humiliated and hungry and broke.

In addition to losing my spouse, half of my friends, and my whole career, I lost material things, such as my home. The twenty-five-hundred-square-foot house sat on a large treed lot in a gated community in Mission Viejo. It boasted twenty-four-foot ceilings and a master bathroom/bedroom/closet combo that was larger than many single-family homes. It was a humbling experience the day I signed my lease on what would be my new abode: an apartment overlooking the 5 Freeway that had no air conditioning, no privacy, and no vibe. My first night in that apartment, I realized if I stood on tiptoe I could touch the popcorn ceiling above. Oh, how I missed those vaulted twenty-fours. I'd gone from the penthouse to the outhouse, in a manner of speaking, and I'd done it in record time.

Given this roller coaster of events, you might think that six months later, when I started making the aforementioned obscene amount of money, I'd have chosen to get out of that up-to-my-eyeballs debt before starting a wild spending spree; but sadly, you'd be wrong. In fact, I blew every last dime of that money on everything *but* servicing my debt. I bought a motorcycle. And then I put a flip-down eight-inch DVD player in my brand new Ford Expedition. And then I put a second *fifteen-inch* DVD player in the back, for children I'd not yet conceived. I'm pretty sure the Bible talks about not being in debt and about giving to the poor and about being a good steward of one's resources and about leaving a worthwhile inheritance for one's children's children. Suffice it to say, I wasn't thinking about all of that.

Here's what I was thinking about instead: Where can I go? What can I do? What can I buy? Hey, what *can't* I buy?

Around the same time I was squandering my newfound wealth, my dad's organization was being audited by the Internal Revenue Service. It used to happen all the time, actually; the ministry he founded had crested annual revenues of $140 million, and the government frequently came to "have a look."

On this occasion, a handful of IRS agents showed up unannounced and declared that they'd need to see summaries of the president's latest dozen or so trips—where had he traveled to, why he had gone, how long he'd stayed, and so forth—as well as the expense reports he'd filed from each one.

Several minutes later, an administrative assistant produced all the requested documentation, handed it over to the agent in charge, and excused herself so that he could review the details. Within seconds, the agent had resurfaced at the assistant's desk, a pressing question on his mind. "Excuse me," he said with a furrowed brow, "but there's a receipt in here from your boss's last trip for a sixty-cent cup of coffee from McDonald's. If I pick through this entire packet, is *this* the kind of stuff I'm going to find?"

The implication of his question was obvious: What senior executive of a hundred-plus-million-dollar organization sees fit to record a sixty-cent cup of joe? Clearly, he hadn't met my dad.

The assistant sheepishly grinned and nodded, to which the agent abruptly said, "We're done here. Thanks for your time." And with that, he rallied his team and left.

My dad was relaying this story to me a short time later, during a conversation we were having about finances. With the massive influx of income I'd been experiencing, I had gone to him seeking advice: Should I incorporate? Should I investigate stocks and bonds? Should I look into various tax shelters for my money, so that my money would keep being mine?

To all my questions, Dad had but one answer: "Ryan," he said, "you can either focus on ministry, or you can focus on money. But you can't do both at once."

He'd go on to explain that there was nothing inherently wrong with looking into Wall Street investments or offshore companies promising safety from excessive taxation, but that in his experience, "dabbling" in such endeavors would take my focus off the work God had called me to do. And that a far less stressful way to live life was to have faith that the God who provided every bit of the income would help me use it to honor Him. He said that the money I was making was somebody's "blood money," the funds they'd otherwise use for housing and clothing and food. "They're contributing their livelihood, Ryan. They are sacrificing cold, hard cash so that we can serve.

"What's more," he said, "that money those contributors keep contributing? *It all belongs to God.* Money isn't ours, Ryan. And money isn't even theirs. All money belongs to God."

Something about his spiel felt familiar, perhaps because I'd heard it ten years before.

For the past thirty-five years a parenting philosophy has gained steam, a philosophy that my dad mastered long before learning to master it was cool. The philosophy is called "Love and Logic" and goes like this: The key to happy interactions between you, the parent, and your child is for you to allow your children to grow through mistakes by letting them experience the natural consequences of the choices they make.

Parents who do the love-and-logic thing well don't get riled up. They don't freak out. They don't threaten or sermonize or bribe. Instead, they simply lay down a set of fair ground rules. They wait for their children to succeed or fail (by all accounts, mostly they fail). And then they let natural consequences run their course.

I'll give you an example of what I mean.

During my first year of college, I'd call home each week to chat with my parents, and inevitably one or both of them would say, "Hey, son, how are your grades?"

My pregnant pause always gave me away.

After a few seconds of uncomfortable silence, my dad would issue the same warning he'd issued week after week after week. In a perfectly calm and love-and-logic-y tone, he'd say, "Ryan, this money isn't ours. This is the Lord's money, money He has entrusted to us to use to build His kingdom. If you choose to waste it, your mom and I will be forced to choose not to supply it to you."

The first few times my dad said those words, secretly, in some teeny tiny place in my heart, I'd think, *There's no way he's serious about this. I mean, he's Dr. James Dobson, child and family psychologist. Suuure, he's going to let his son get kicked out of college . . . not to mention a Christian college.* [I was at Olivet Nazarene University at the time; this was before my Biola days.] *Sure, he'll let his son get booted from here. Yeah, right. In your dreams!*

Imagine my shock and awe when he actually made good on his word.

At the end of that particular semester, and upon learning that my grades in fact had not improved, my dad totally cut me off. He called me on the phone and in that same annoyingly measured tone said, "Ryan, I'm sorry, son. I don't want to have to do this, but I made a promise to you, and if I don't keep that promise, I become a liar. Your grades are still too low, which means I no longer can pay for your schooling. Oh, and you may not come home, either."

There it was, in two minutes flat.

No more money.

No more school.

No more *nothing*.

Thank you, and have a nice day.

I was floored. Dr. James Dobson, child and family psychologist, had in effect kicked his son out of school—a scandal, if ever there were one, right? Scandalous is certainly how it felt to me.

At the time, MTV had just begun production for a show they called *The Real World,* a reality TV show in which a bunch of single adults were thrown together from different backgrounds, different parts of the country, and different life experiences. They were to live for three months' time within the same four walls of a California mansion while upward of thirty cameras recorded their every move, every hour of the day. I watched the first episode of *The Real World* on the tiny TV in the living room of the place where I was paying rent.

The real estate company had called my place a "cottage" in the for-rent listing, but in actuality it was a one-hundred-year-old hovel with a foundation so problematic that the left side of the building sat about thirty degrees lower than the right. To make matters worse, instead of shoring up the structure the owners simply had lopped off the upper third of the door at that same thirty-degree angle, causing my front door to bear an eerie resemblance to the top of Gumby's head. I could touch all four walls of my living room by stretching out my arms to the left and to the right and pivoting ninety degrees, and I distinctly remember seeing those "real world" singles living it up in a mansion with nary a care in the world and saying, "No, no, no. *That* is not the real world. *This*—this cottage, this being kicked out of school, this nowhere to go and nothing worthwhile to do—*this right here* is what we call *the real world.*"

I didn't care for the real world one bit.

It was wintertime then, as I recall. And freezing cold, at least for this Californian. I'd wake every morning, rush into the living room, and stand in front of the miniscule wall heater mounted in a corner of the living room, and jog in place in a futile attempt to get warm. But as awful as things were for me, I now know they were far, far worse for my dad. Because he *was*, in fact, Dr. James

Dobson, child and family psychologist. And he was the loving father of a louse of a son.

I sometimes think about all those board meetings my dad had to attend during those years. I envision him walking into the board room dressed in suit and tie, prepared for weighty discussions about meaningful goings-on in the organization's life, and engaging in pre-meeting banter with the other board members, who inevitably would ask, "So, how are your kids, Jim?" I then picture my dad, poor guy, working desperately to hedge: "Good! Really good. Danae is writing her nineteenth book and is doing really, really well."

He'd look for a way to then shift the conversation, even as he knew he'd surely be caught. But then of course the next question would surface, much to my dad's chagrin. "And how's Ryan?" the other board member would say, even as another little piece of my dad's heart died.

Ryan. What to say about Ryan.

The truth was never an easy pill to choke down: "Well, Ryan fooled around in school and wasted so much money that he forced me to pull him out. He's in a dead-end job working for a boss he doesn't respect, he lives in near-squalor in an unsafe part of town, and he's not really motivated to make much more of his life. That's exactly how Ryan is."

When I was fifteen or sixteen years old, I happened to be sitting in my dad's home office—he called it his "den"—when the local news came on TV. The evening anchor was describing how Jim and Tammy Faye Bakker's woes were only mounting, now that their televangelism ministry, "The PTL Club"—standing for

"Praise the Lord"—was falling apart. Government officials had determined the Bakkers had engaged in fraudulent accounting practices and now were seizing all their worldly possessions—homes, cars, boats, jewelry, air-conditioned dog houses, and more. As video footage ran of those belongings being carted away from the Bakkers' home, my dad turned to me and said, "You will *never* see me involved in something like that. *Ever.*"

I had no context for the Bakkers' dilemma, nor did I fully understand the passion in my father's voice. But the memory has stuck with me all these years; and now that I'm a businessman and a husband and a dad myself, I get what he was declaring there in that den. He was saying, "All the seemingly insignificant things I do regarding money—budgeting carefully, watching our spending, being accountable for each and every dime . . . they're going to matter in the end."

Along the way naysayers would accuse my dad of opulent living, of having too nice a car, too big a dining-room table, too lavish a vacation, but what those thin charges failed to take into consideration was that my dad never once took a salary in exchange for the work he did year after year. He never took book proceeds and spoiled his two children with brand new BMWs, although a teeny tiny part of me wishes he would have.

Instead, he produced great content in the form of books and CDs and films, and he chose to live off the earnings from that revenue stream instead of eyeing his ministry for salaried cash. What's more, on day one of his ministry career, he sorted out a dollar amount he needed to live on and then gave *every penny* after that away. He practices the same approach today.

On occasion, I'd come across one of those naysayers' comments and would carefully watch how my dad chose to respond. Personally, I thought my dad should be able to drive whatever car he wanted to drive, just like the rest of the free world. "If they take issue with your vehicle of choice, that's their problem!" I'd puff out my chest and rant. But he saw things a shade differently. "Yes. Maybe it *is* their problem," he would say. "But Ryan, it's my problem too."

He never wanted to compromise his message by being perceived as an irresponsible messenger. The older I get, the more I realize there's some wisdom to living this way.

Two summers ago a wildfire broke out in a canyon not far from my family's home. Within three days, the fire had jumped yet another canyon and was now racing down the side of the hill that abuts our property. It was terrifying. I was running through the house like a crazy person, grabbing our computers, our external hard drives, a few family photos, and my favorite guns, when this thought occurred to me: *the rest of this stuff is just stuff.*

In the midst of an ever-darkening sky due to massive amounts of smoke and ash utterly filling the atmosphere, I actually sensed real refreshment, like when you're inhaling cool, crisp air. Sure, I'd miss the things that made our home feel like home. And I'd miss the extensive vinyl-record collection Laura and I have built across the last eight years. But as I darted in and out of each room of our house, I realized none of our treasured belongings would amount to anything in the end.

Four days following that fire, and while my family and I still were evacuated to another part of town, we were told by city officials that our home had been deemed a "total loss." In fact, more than three hundred and fifty homes in our area were burned to the ground, so we weren't exactly shocked by the news. I think my verbatim response was, "Huh. How about that."

Yes, life would be inconvenient for a while, but since when is convenience the goal? I looked at Laura and at Lincoln and Luci and thought, *All I really care about is still here.*

We would learn on day five following the fire that there had been a mistake in the city's reporting, that our home had fared okay after all. But that was neither here nor there; we'd learned about ourselves what we needed to know. Our house didn't have a hold on us. We were grateful for its shelter but were unfazed when we'd thought it had been lost. I saw this progress for what it was. My dad's approach to money was taking effect in my heart. I looked at things differently now.

The first few years after Laura and I were married, we clawed our way out of debt by selling belongings and tightening our spending habits. When it was time to buy a home, we consulted my dad for wisdom and then actually took his advice in the end. He had come by to walk through each of the two homes we were considering buying, one of which was far more expensive than the other. And in his endlessly diplomatic way, he looked at me and said of that bigger, better, nicer, more tempting purchase, "Ryan, I think you'll regret spending this much money on a house."

I thought back on how I'd bucked even conventional wisdom regarding home ownership before, about how despite what experts say about spending no more than 25 percent of your take-home income on housing, I'd easily dropped 110 percent each month to own my "dream home" all those miserable years ago. Of course I hadn't *owned* a dream home; I'd owned an exorbitant mortgage at best. Would I make the same mistake twice?

One week later, Laura and I took possession of the not-as-big, not-as-nice house, and we've never once regretted the move. Our mortgage is microscopic, and we are living free for the first time in years. The Bible talks about wise men building their house upon a rock instead of on shifting sand. If the "rock" represents financial prudence, then maybe I was becoming a wise man after all.

I was at the grocery store last week and noticed there on the clearance aisle a really nice molded-plastic Darth Vader mask, left over from their Halloween push. My son loves Darth Vader, and I fantasized briefly about presenting him with that mask and then watching him freak out with childish delight. The little tag on it read $4.99.

Five bucks.

What's five bucks—especially since Lincoln is so appreciative of *any* gift?

My kid would have hugged me and thanked me and called me Blessed Father for an entire month over that mask. But still, I didn't buy the mask. I didn't buy the mask because I'm trying to practice a principle that was important to my dad and that is becoming increasingly important to me: *I will live as though money isn't mine; all money belongs to God.*

You know what I whispered as I left that sale aisle? "Thank you" is what I said. Although he wasn't there, I was whispering it to my dad.

Thank you for teaching me the value of five bucks.

Thank you for modeling for me accountability for every dime.

Thank you for showing me how to live with a contented heart.

Thank you for helping me learn that special occasions are only special because you haven't bought every five-dollar Darth Vader mask that comes along.

My son is seven. He doesn't fully "get" money yet. But I can promise you he's learning. He sees the little Dave Ramsey piggy banks in his room and knows that every dollar that comes his way must make room for savings and giving and a tithe. He is presented with a treat from Mom or Dad and knows it is *very special*; treats don't happen every day. He hears me talk about how grateful I am for those who contribute to my dad's and my radio ministry—"Lincoln, that's *blood money* they're giving to us!"—and little seeds get planted in his mind and heart that will bloom into responsibility someday.

I'm not perfect here, but I'm better.

I'm better at living as though money isn't mine.

finding your exceptional life

1. When have you defied financial wisdom in your own life? What have the results of your negligence been?

2. What do you wish were true of you, on the money-management front?

3. What promises of God can you claim in helping create reality from that dream?

4

rolling the dice

You have to risk going too far to discover
just how far you can really go.

—T. S. Eliot

My dad has a time-tested, proven philosophy for successful living that I've always found nearly impossible to accept. "You roll the dice enough times," he'd say, "you'll eventually come up snake eyes." The implied takeaway here, of course, was, "Think twice before rolling those dice."

Clearly, this philosophy was crafted by a man who wasn't born with adrenaline flowing through his veins. I'm forty-three years old now and learned only in the last two years' time that being taken to the emergency room nearly forty times isn't a normal, natural, even enjoyable part of everyone's adolescent lives. For

me the ER was a second home, thanks to the antics that left my
parents shaking their heads, and also, I'm sure, kneeling at their
bedside in prayer.

I'd free-climb two-story buildings and "surf" atop various
vehicles in motion and jump my pickup truck twenty feet in the
air across a fifty-foot chasm, not fully appreciating that this is
typically an axle-busting activity. I'd enter California's 5 Freeway
nearly every time with one thought in mind: *I wonder how fast I
can get to 100 mph*. And I did these things not once, but hundreds
upon hundreds of times.

I'd try to keep up with my bike-riding friends while on an
admittedly slower skateboard; and on one especially painful occasion, I did a full-on belly slide. My buddies had already crossed
the busy intersection, and so I was pushing as fast as I could, not
realizing that at the point at which the sidewalk met the cross-
street there was a divot in the pavement about the same width as
the width of my board's front wheels. I went from full speed to
no speed in a matter of seconds, and while my board stopped, its
front axle firmly planted in that divot, my body lurched forward
into midair and then landed—hands, torso, and eventually legs
skidding along twenty feet of the street.

There I was, lying there face down, blood pouring from everywhere, as a whole string of people looked on. They were waiting
in line for a table at the corner café and had the audacity to *stay in
line*. I began surveying the damage as my friends, who did finally
realize I hadn't kept up with them, turned around and pedaled
back. Parts of me were missing: the palms of my hands, the pads
on my elbows, the soft flesh that had once covered my hipbones,
the tops of both knees. My buddies helped me slowly rise to my

feet and steadied me as I hobbled over to the curb. I passed the gawking onlookers and yelled, "I can't believe none of you came to help me!"

Where was a Good Samaritan when you needed one?

I was thirteen years old at the time, and while I'm sure my parents expected me to find another less painful activity besides skateboarding to occupy me from that point forward, within a week, I was back out there skating empty swimming pools and honing my tricks.

Comedian Jerry Seinfeld once said that whenever he's driving around Los Angeles and happens to see skaters at a skate park or riding stair rails, he thinks, *You know, they're going to be okay. Those guys will make it in life.*

His rationale is based on the fact that in order to do the tricks those guys are doing, they've had to throw their bodies into very painful positions over and over again, day after day, week after week, month after agonizing month. Who else takes risks like that, choosing to *injure* themselves all the time? He's onto something, I think.

I caught an interview one time between Tony Hawk and Rodney Mullen, two men who revolutionized skateboarding in the 1980s and 1990s, and Rodney was talking about a hip injury he'd sustained. The hip was out of joint, hanging on by nothing but scar tissue, and when he'd skate and try to do tricks, the hip would seize up on him. The only relief to be found, he said, was to lie down on the street underneath his car, fold his leg up into the wheel well, move the leg until his hip hitched, and then violently jerk it back into place. He would be screaming and crying while he did this to himself, and on one occasion an onlooker called the

cops, thinking this poor guy was actually stuck in the undercar-
riage of a car.

Skate or die, right? Rodney's autobiography is aptly titled *How
to Skateboard and Not Kill Yourself.* He ought to know; he's walked
that line a thousand times.

Now, my dad would read an account like that and say, "Why
tempt fate that way?" He would see cockiness or arrogance where
I see only a thrill-seeker in search of a thrill. Plus, those of us who
make a habit of doing what saner people call "stupid things" share
a pervasive belief that we'll be okay in the end. Sure, there may be
broken bones or lots of blood or lengthy hospital stays, but everything will work itself out eventually, we're certain. Over time, we'll
bounce right back.

I would get to the point where I could even spiritualize it,
believing that since God was a God of rescue—à la the Israelites
and David and Daniel—if I got myself into trouble accidentally,
of course He would rescue me. I failed to take into account that
the Bible more often refers to God's *willingness* or His *ability* to
rescue and not necessarily His *decision* to do so. It was this minor
oversight that was brought to my attention during the intervention
my family staged on my behalf.

I started riding motorcycles at the recommendation of a
counselor I was seeing during a real low point in my life. Betty
said, "Ryan, you can't look to other people to make you happy.
Happiness is your responsibility. And while you're walking
through this decidedly unhappy season, my suggestion is that you
find something that brings you joy and then carve out intentional
time to do that thing, as a way to keep your spirits up."

And so I bought a bike.

This is why it was so upsetting to me when I showed up for Thanksgiving dinner nearly a decade ago to find my dad, my dad's cousin, my mom, and various other extended family members loaded for bear. The topic: motorcycle riding. The target, unfortunately: me.

My dad had worked the ER years prior, when he was doing rounds to earn his Ph.D. in California, and he had seen far too much. My mom was in full support of my dad's position, believing nothing good could come from my riding a bike. My dad's cousin, Bill, may he rest in peace, was quite possibly the most brilliant person I've ever known. With an IQ of two hundred and street smarts to match, I knew that while he'd surely take my parents' side on this matter, I had to at least hear him out.

According to smart people who spend their time studying and reporting the primary causes of motorcycle crashes, there are five reasons bikes go down. The rider either fails to properly negotiate a left-hand bend in the road; he fails to properly negotiate a right-hand bend in the road; he suffers a collision at a junction; he suffers a collision while trying to pass another vehicle; or he simply loses control.

These causes aren't surprising; what is surprising is how often they occur. The same smart people who assess the reasons for crashes also assess their frequency, and they have determined that the percentage likelihood of your being in a motorcycle accident if a motorcycle is your daily mode of transportation is not 50 percent or even 75 percent. It's 100 percent, which is why so many insurance companies refuse to provide coverage for bikers.

This would not bode well for me on intervention day.

There are all sorts of things you can do to avoid having a motorcycle crash. You can make sure you're well trained, for instance. You can wear a helmet and reflective clothing. You can approach intersections cautiously. You can keep your distance from other vehicles and never travel side-by-side with other riders and stay home at the first sight of rain. Or, you can do as my father was suggesting that Thanksgiving day: "Come to your senses and quit riding that bike!"

My dad and his cousin laid out for me the inevitable risks of riding, citing the doom-and-gloom you're-surely-going-to-die statistics they'd secured, and upon hearing all of this information, two thoughts occurred to me. First, I thought about how all this talk of bikes kind of made me want to excuse myself and go for a ride. And second, I thought, *If anyone can beat those downer stats, it'll be me.*

When I reengaged in the conversation at hand, I heard my dad pipe up with the exact words I expected him to say: "If you keep rolling the dice, Ryan, eventually they'll come up snake eyes."

Laura and I were married on June 12, 2005, and soon afterward, I had a revelation. I like being married to this woman. Furthermore, I wanted to grow old with this woman. And that's when it hit me: I can't grow old with this woman I like if I get myself killed doing stupid things.

The revelation wouldn't stop me from paying a commercial fishing company to take us on a shark feed during vacation one time and then, just as the sharks were being whipped into a feeding frenzy by the slapping of raw meat on the surface of the water, sticking my hand through the cage we were swimming inside to "pet" the very cool shark. But it would cause later self-reflection. My rationale at the time seemed sound enough to me: this was a commercial enterprise that couldn't stay in business if tourists were dying from shark bites every other week. Furthermore, if I had been the single tourist to get chomped on, what a great story I'd have to tell!

The self-reflective part was realizing that while it was a story I'd have a ball telling, it would have definite implications for my wife. For starters, she'd be terrified as the whole thing went down. Then, assuming I survived, I would be out of work for a bit. There would be surgeries I'd have to recover from, and the inconvenience of it all would rest on her. *I like this woman. I want to grow old with this woman. I don't want to be known for doing stupid things.*

Not too long after that revelation, Laura delivered our first baby, a beautiful baby boy we named Lincoln Cash, which only served to cement my don't-be-stupid resolve. What my newfound maturity was showing me is just how selfish recklessness can be. There is a time and a place for risk-taking, but I could see how making those times fewer and farther between and those places not quite so ubiquitous would definitely serve my family well. As usual, my dad had been right: Dice-rollers eventually find snake eyes—it wasn't an *if,* but a *when.*

I was in my mid-thirties by then and had some perspective on things. I started thinking about my dad's lifelong practice as a tee-totaler, for instance, and began to see his abstinence as a wisdom-play. "Can people drink alcohol and not have a problem?" he'd say to me rhetorically. "Of course. And, *you don't know if you're one of them.* To drink is to willfully roll the dice."

I thought about my dad suffering a full-on heart attack and then, after his recovery, becoming absolutely religious about maintaining healthful patterns on the diet and exercise fronts. He was on his treadmill daily, you couldn't pay him to touch a doughnut, and wherever he traveled he made sure a portable defibrillator was along, in case something unexpected went down.

How would I have felt if he had shirked these responsibilities and simply thrown caution to the wind, if he'd been flippant and reckless instead?

I knew what my honest answer meant for me. A little circumspection, perhaps. For once.

Yes, I still push the envelope every once in a while—especially if the rental car has but thirteen miles on it and nobody's on the road. (The speeding ticket was worth it, by the way. Old habits die really hard.) Yes, I'd hop on a bike again in a heartbeat, if I could guarantee I wouldn't get killed. Yes, I still staple the Christmas lights to our house by dangling my body upside-down with nothing but the lip of the vent on the roof anchoring my toes. Yes, I still answer Laura's parting comment nearly every time I leave the house—"Be safe, honey"—with a defiant, "I won't. But I'll try not to get hurt." But the truth is, I've been softened—by wisdom, by time, by love. I want to be here as long as possible to enjoy the most enjoyable people I know.

finding your exceptional life

1. What has "riskiness" looked like in your life so far? How do you know when you're pushing the envelope too far?

2. What do you make of the assertion that recklessness is at its core a selfish endeavor?

3. What type of risk-taking do you find in the life of Jesus, during His ministry here on earth? What would compel you to take similar risks?

5

be there

To see the world in a grain of sand, and to see
heaven in a wild flower, hold infinity in the palm
of your hands, and eternity in an hour.

—WILLIAM BLAKE

On January 5, 1988, Peter "Pistol Pete" Maravich, star of LSU's late-1960's basketball teams, college basketball's all-time scoring leader still today, one of the youngest players ever inducted into the NBA Hall of Fame, and the guy the Hall called perhaps the greatest creative offensive talent in history—suddenly dropped dead. He was only forty years old.

It's a date my dad never will forget because he was the one administering CPR just after Pete Maravich breathed his last breath.

Pistol Pete got his name during his high-school days because of the way he shot the ball. He fired it from his hip, as though he was holding a revolver, and although the movement was unorthodox, it seemed to work out fine for him. The guy could *play*. That is, until he couldn't. As is the case for many professional athletes, injuries shortened Pete's NBA career, forcing him to retire at age thirty-three. Seven years later, he boarded a plane for Los Angeles, where he had agreed to be a guest on my dad's radio show. Maravich was a born-again Christian and was excited to talk with listeners about his faith.

For years prior to that occasion, my dad had served as the unofficial organizer of a four-on-four pickup game of basketball, held three mornings a week at a local church gym. He thought it would be fun for Maravich to play with the group during a special Tuesday-morning game. After forty-five minutes or so, the men took a break, and my dad asked Maravich how he was feeling. Pistol Pete said, "I feel great!" He then talked about how much he loved the game of basketball and about how he really should find a way to play more often, even in spite of his nagging shoulder injury. My dad agreed with him, and then the two of them shared a laugh over something, and then in the blink of an eye, Pete Maravich crashed to the floor, felled by a rare congenital heart defect. It was so sudden and so dramatic that he couldn't even brace his own fall.

My father arrived home late that morning and was visibly shaken. He got right in my face and said, "Ryan, Pete died today, and I had to be the one to call his family and let them know. He was feeling great and doing well one minute, and then *the very next minute* he was gone."

I'd never known my dad to have such urgency in his voice. Whatever had happened in the gym that morning had rattled him to his core.

"I may not get another opportunity to say this to you, Ryan," my dad continued, "so I'll say it now. When I cross over to the other side, *be there*. You've got to assure me that you'll be there."

I was eighteen years old at the time and had absolutely zero tolerance for discussions about mortality—especially my dad's. I think I nodded dumbfoundedly in response to my father's impassioned plea and then quickly changed the subject.

Two years later, on that very same basketball court, my dad was the one in crisis. He'd had a full-blown heart attack but in typical Dr. James Dobson style had driven himself to the hospital. I was at home, still asleep, when my mom rushed into my bedroom and said, "Ryan, get up. Get up!"

My first bleary-eyed thought was, *This had better be good.*

As I raced to the ER, my mom trying to stay calm in the passenger seat, I silently prayed desperate prayers: "Lord, please let him live long enough for me to see him, for me at least to say good-bye . . ."

Just then my mom was saying, "Ryan, *slow down*. I don't want to lose *both* of you in *one* day." This is where we go in a crisis, isn't it . . . we try to control whatever small things we can.

My mom and I walked into Dad's room in the intensive-care unit, where he had been transferred, and found him lying there looking very vulnerable in a hospital gown with tubes flowing from his nose and sensors plastered all over his body. My breath hitched as I took him in. I'd never seen him look so awful; was this really the end for him? In that moment all I could think about was the long line of heart disease in Dobson men, and now the odds here suddenly didn't feel good. My dad's dad was simply enjoying dinner with my grandma, when he leaned over and rested his head on her shoulder. Thinking he was just goofing around, she said, "Honey, what are you doing?" to which he replied . . . nothing. He was already in heaven. I drew in a deep breath as I stood before my dad, fearful he too would pass before my eyes.

My father's breathing was labored, but he was coherent, and after a moment or two he locked eyes with me. "Ryan," he whispered, "you've got to be there, son. Tell me that you'll be there."

We were going to do this *again*?

"There is nothing more important than keeping that appointment, Ry," he continued. "You've got to assure me that you'll be there."

Something in me wanted to scream, "Quit talking about this, Dad! Hey, *here's* an idea. How about you focus on *living*, instead of on *dying*. How about instead of telling me to *be there*, you just *stay here*?"

Years ago, my dad and his colleagues went around the country hosting conferences for families, and they'd always end the final session the same way, with the "be there" challenge. Participants could even take a pledge, which served as something of a living will for their families. In effect, the pledge told their loved ones that they had made a heartfelt commitment to following Jesus Christ and that yes, they would definitely "be there" someday—"there," of course, meaning heaven.

I always felt resentful of that pledge. Frankly, I didn't want to talk about such things. I was struggling enough with the idea of life; why on earth would I invite thoughts of *death*?

What I couldn't possibly understand as an invincible teenager that I am starting now to grasp is that there really is no greater joy than to know that your children are walking in truth; that you'll never have to say good-bye because you'll be with them eternally. All those "be there" exhortations from my dad were his way of saying, "Listen, I know you say God is an important part of your life, but I want to make sure He *is* your life. I don't want any ambiguity here; I want to know we'll be together—you and me—forever."

A few nights ago my family and I were walking home from the park, when Laura and Lincoln decided to race each other the rest of the way. Part of me relished the sight of my wife and my boy running like the wind, taunting each other and laughing with each other and looking as though they had not a care in the world. But for another part of me, there was a wince. I know this kid. I know how he runs. I know he never looks where he's going and that most days he's just *asking* to crash and burn.

I quickened my pace there behind Luci's stroller to try to close the distance between us and them, hollering, "Keep your eyes on what's in front of you, Lincoln!" to nobody but the stiff breeze.

Reflexively I flashed back to when I myself was a kid, smaller than Lincoln even, and took my first trip to the ER. I'd wanted to see how far I could run across the backyard with my eyes closed. I remember thinking, *This will be so cool! I wonder how far I can go!*

As it turned out, I didn't go very far.

After fifteen or twenty paces, my full-speed attempt was interrupted by a metal spike used for gardening, which split my head open in two. It hurt. I remember it hurting. I remember my mom rushing outside and screaming at the pool of blood and rushing back inside to grab a stack of dish towels and then rushing back out to gather me up.

Thirteen stitches I got that day, just above my left eye. The doctor told my mom that had the stake implanted itself a quarter-inch lower, it would have killed me. Between the numbing shot that made me woozy, the threading of my head that seemed to touch my skull, and the massive headache that ensued, I was in a sorry state. Running blind wasn't cool after all.

My dad had been out to lunch with a friend when it happened, and so my mom had frantically scribbled a note on Dad's Children's Hospital Los Angeles stationery and left it on the desk in his den. I know this because my dad saves *everything*, including the note informing him his son had made a teeny tiny mistake and now was being rushed to the hospital because there was an alarming amount of blood rushing from his little face.

A friend of my father's had picked him up for their lunch appointment, and my dad hadn't thought to grab his set of keys upon leaving, mostly because my mom was supposed to be home all afternoon preparing for a garage sale we were having the next day. He rang the doorbell, but of course nobody answered, and so he found a way into the garage, located a ladder, positioned it outside the master-bedroom window, and jimmied it open. He later told me that before climbing through the window, he happened to peek through the downstairs window that looked into his den, where he saw the note from my mom on his otherwise perfectly clean desk.

From his vantage point the note was upside-down, but he quickly made out what it said. And according to him, he's never made better time to the hospital than he did that particular afternoon.

That entire scene came rushing back to mind about a month ago, when my family was enjoying a lazy afternoon at my parents' house. They live in a condo overlooking a golf course and have a beautiful brick patio that runs along the back of their place. My dad and Lincoln love to play together, and on that day, the game was tag. My dad had a rubber ball the size of a soccer ball and would chase Lincoln with it until he could lob it at my son's legs or feet, tagging him and making him "it." My dad would then take off running, and Lincoln would be right on his heels, belly-laughing and hollering his boyish threats at my dad, "I'm gonna get you! Here I come!"

My mom, Laura, and I were sitting on the patio with baby Luci, relishing in the tag-team's banter, when I saw Lincoln flash by me like a bullet, with my dad hot on his tail. My son was running at full speed, as fast as those little legs would go, and then in the split second it took for his flight to be arrested, he was running fast no more. Lincoln had crashed his entire body into a large brick planter, effectively whipping his face against stone and spearing his torso with the planter's sharp edge.

I had been right there, at arm's length of my son, and yet there was nothing I could have done. Springing from my seat and rushing to him, I mentally prepared myself for the worst: broken jaw, broken teeth, cracked orbital bone, cracked ribs. When I got to the "cracked ribs" part of my hypothetical assessment, I began to totally freak out. *What if he punctured his heart or his lungs? Is my son going to be okay?*

A little piece of me died there on the spot, as I reached down to gather up my kid.

Lincoln was wailing and moaning gutturally—I'd never heard him cry like that—as I hurried him into the house and laid him gently on my parents' bed. Gathering up my courage, I began to carefully look him over, head to toe. There was a small scrape on his knee . . . and was that a bruise forming on his chest? But, wait. Was that *it*? A scrape and an easy bruise?

In the end, Lincoln would walk away totally unharmed.

I, on the other hand, was a mess. This is why I winced when Laura and Lincoln were racing home last week, because Lincoln never looks where he's going, and because Lincoln has absolutely taken my breath away with some of his spills, and because life is fragile and tragic accidents happen and *that little boy is my heart.*

Life has a way of delivering up reminders that you and I aren't home yet. We tend to forget this truth. We sign thirty-year mortgages and purchase lifetime warranties and make ourselves comfortable in every possible way. But the truth? It's that we're sojourners; this world isn't a permanent place. This is what my dad was hinting at, back when he was recovering in the ICU. He was saying, "Ryan, the day will come when I'm not here anymore, but that doesn't have to be the end. Our deal—yours and mine? It can go on forever, son. We can live eternally side by side."

Life threw my dad a curve ball, by way of a devastating, full-on stroke. Right in front of my mom, he was rendered impotent—no speech, no recognition, full paralysis. He was leveled, and my family was scared, but astoundingly, he'd bounce back again.

Three days later, thanks to a massive anticoagulant, we were talking on the phone like nothing had happened.

But the point of all of it certainly wasn't lost on me, which is that this life that's full of twists and turns leaves us twisted up and totally turned around. Sure, we can control the small stuff—where we work, where we live, what we eat, what we wear. But the big stuff? It's out of our hands. Peacemakers can't *make* wars end, financial managers can't *make* a recession go away, and parents can't *make* their prodigal children come home. I think about this last one a lot. To pray for a baby and birth a baby and then lovingly raise that child, to teach him about life and about love and about God and then be forced to watch him simply walk away . . . I imagine this is a special sort of agony for a parent, the realization that the one who shares your history and your name may not be with you all your days.

The best we can do, I think, is exactly what my dad always has done: keep inviting our kids to stay by our side. "Be there, Ryan," he'd implore me. "You've got to tell me that you will be there." We invite them, and then we intercede for them, remembering that even the thief on the cross got to "be there," despite his rejection of God for most of his life. Luke 23 says that when Jesus Christ was crucified on the place called Skull Hill, two criminals were also killed that day. One of the men hurled insults at Jesus, but the other was humbled by Christ's presence and asked to "be remembered" when Jesus came into His kingdom—he was making a plea here for eternal life.

Jesus' response was totally shocking and also not surprising at all. The long-suffering God incarnate said, "I tell you the truth, today you will be with me in paradise" (v. 43).

And so we pray. We pray knowing that bodies are fragile and that fleeting is our time here on earth . . . and we pray believing that God is in the business of redemption and that even hardened criminals wind up coming to Christ.

We pray that we and all those we adore would learn to "number our days aright," as Psalm 90:12 says, "that we may gain a heart of wisdom."

We don't know how long we have here, do we? May we wisely approach our days.

Years ago, my sister Danae had a plaque made for my dad and inscribed it with his oft-spoken two-word phrase: *Be there.* It was her way of saying, "I know this is of utmost importance to you, Dad, and I want you to know it's important to me too."

I was upstairs in my dad's office at the radio studio just this morning and saw it there on his bookshelf, where it has rested all this time. I picked it up off its little wooden easel, I brushed off the fine layer of dust that is always present here in arid Colorado, and I slowly ran my thumb across the jagged edges of those engraved words. I exhaled a breath of gratitude—that Dad will always be there and, by God's grace, I'll be there too.

finding your exceptional life

1. How would you respond if a loved one pleaded for you to "be there"—to be in heaven someday?

2. When do you most feel the fragile, fleeting nature of this life?

3. Why is it so easy to get caught up in the things of this world, when we know this is not our permanent home?

6

little things matter

Don't marry the person you think you can live with; marry only the individual you think you can't live without.

—James C. Dobson

For the first thirty-seven years of my life, I had an intestinal disorder that caused me to convulsively throw up every four to six weeks, like clockwork. I don't mean I'd throw up once or twice each time; I mean I would vomit compulsively, nonstop, for days on end. One time in my late twenties, I lost eleven pounds in two days. I'm not a large man; this was a significant amount of weight.

Most people who get migraines get them in their head, but my migraines came in my gut, which would cause it to seize up, which then would inflict crazy amounts of pain and suffering on me. Many times, the "event," as I came to call it, landed me in the emergency room; *every* time, the event was grim. I couldn't eat. I couldn't sleep. I could barely stand on my own two feet, hence all those horrific hospital visits. They knew me there by name.

During year thirty-eight of my life, "they"—meaning all the doctors and specialists and smart people who get paid big bucks to sort out problematic health realities but who for some reason could not find a diagnosis for me for more than three decades' time—finally determined that I had ulcerative colitis and a rip in my stomach and a whole lot of issues I'd contend with the rest my life.

My dad worked at Children's Hospital LA for many years and had unofficially diagnosed me long before that. He had taken me to twelve or thirteen upper-GI specialists in his quest to cure what ailed me; but it would take more tests, more research, more analysis, more input, before a way out could be declared.

The eventual answer, the thing that would save me from suffering further vomiting bouts across the decades I'd not yet lived, the solution to the thirty-plus-year problem, was a teeny tiny pill. It was a mild *muscle relaxer*, of all things, a simple fix for a complex issue, a bit of salvation no larger than the nail on my pinky finger. At last: I had a way out.

All those times when I would get sicker than sick, a certain headache would tip me off. If that particular headache started to rise up from my neck, I'd know I'd better find a bucket, and fast. Now all I had to do when the headache emerged was find my pill bottle instead. No harmful ingredients. No lasting side effects. Nothing but goodness in those tiny little pills: bing, bang, boom.

Now. This happens to be a chapter on marriage, which I know at this moment doesn't seem to square. Hang with me for a moment, and it will.

If you'll recall, I mentioned previously that, at thirty years old, I went through a divorce. And for a while, I was so depressed and forlorn that I couldn't see the nose in front of my face, let alone make astute observations about the life that was continuing on without me. But once I did emerge from the haze, from the awfulness that is being married and then suddenly being unmarried, it occurred to me that perhaps I'd been doing marriage all wrong. This thought occurred to me because perhaps for the first time I noticed how very right my parents' marriage was. For starters, they enjoyed being together. Profound, right? You could give them a whole slew of fantastic options for what to do with a given day, and they'd pick "just be together" every time. Every. Single. Time.

It was a little thing, admittedly, but so was my little pill. Do little things have a way of adding up? They do. I knew beyond a doubt that they do.

During that season when I was trying to put my life back together again, I had a front-row seat into their lives, and what I saw was compelling and sweet. By this point they had mastered the little things, and those little things equaled something big.

My dad was never a natural romantic. It wasn't that he was opposed to it; it's just that it tended to slip his mind. Case in point: when my parents were first married, my dad accidentally worked late on February 14. This was well before the invention of cell phones, and so when he finally left the office and headed over to his parents' house for a quick drop-in visit, my mom was left home, unaware.

When he entered his parents' home, his mother offered to "fix him a plate." It was late, and my dad was hungry, and so without thinking, he sat down and ate. Again, my mom was home, alone, completely oblivious to things.

Eventually, having chatted and enjoyed dinner and made his way back to his car, my dad drove the few miles to his own house, where my unaware, oblivious mother was crossing the threshold between anger and rage. Where had my father *been* all this time? And on *Valentine's Day*, no less? My mom was fit to be tied.

Now my father was the completely oblivious one, but reality would soon dawn on him. He entered the house and saw there on the dining room table two plates filled with food that was now cold and one candle that had burned down to a nub. Here he was, a clinical psychologist, a *professional student of human behavior*, and yet he'd unwittingly infuriated the most important human in his life, the woman who now was silently crying in bed with the covers pulled over her head.

"It was all a surprise," my dad later would plead, saying he'd had no clue it was Valentine's Day. Even his parents had failed to mention the holiday, when he'd spent a few hours with them that night, but they weren't the best in the romance department either; they may not have known it had even come.

Of course my mom forgave him, and of course they moved on from that night. But it had a lasting impact on my dad, who became a self-trained romantic on par with Saint Valentine himself.

Eons later, during a weekend retreat some twenty years into their marriage, my dad stole away in a room of the hotel where he and my mom were staying one morning to write a letter to his bride. "Who else shares the memory of my youth during which the foundations of love were laid?" he began. "I ask you, who else could occupy the place that is reserved for the only woman who was there when I graduated from college and went to the Army and returned as a student at USC and bought my first decent car (and promptly wrecked it) and picked out an inexpensive wedding ring with you (and paid for it with Savings Bonds), and we prayed and thanked God for what we had.

"Then we said the wedding vows and my dad prayed, 'Lord, You gave us Jimmy and Shirley as infants to love and cherish and raise for a season, and tonight, we give them back to You after our labor of love—not as two separate individuals, but as one.' And everyone cried.

"Then we left for our honeymoon and spent all our money and came home to an apartment full of rice and a bell on the bed, and we had only just begun."

My dad continued recounting their lifetime of shared experiences—the classes they taught, the first home they bought, the accidental planting of a veritable forest in their front yard, their first "real" salary, my mom's first ski accident, the birth of their two children, the beginnings of their ministry (which a three-year-old listener fondly referred to as "Poke Us in the Fanny"), the ups and downs and the twists and turns and the book deals and ordeals and trips—and then concluded his letter this way:

> So I ask you! Who's gonna take your place in my life? You have become me and I have become you. . . . Is it any wonder that I can read your face like a book when we are in a crowd? The slightest narrowing of your eyes speaks volumes to me about the thoughts that are running through your conscious experience. As you open Christmas presents, I know instantly if you like the color

or the style of the gift, because your feelings cannot be hidden from me.

I love you, S.M.D. I love the girl who believed in me before I believed in myself. I love the girl who never complained about huge school bills and books and hot apartments and rented junky furniture and no vacations and humble little Volkswagens. You have been with me— encouraging me, loving me, and supporting me since August 27, 1960. And the status you have given me in our home is beyond what I have deserved.

So why do I want to go on living? It's because I have you to take the journey with. Otherwise, why make the trip? . . . The only joy of the future will be in experiencing it as we have the past twenty-one years—hand in hand with the one I love . . . a young miss named Shirley Deere, who gave me everything she had—including her heart.[3]

Hello! Romantic, right? He taught himself to practice romance because romance matters to my mom. Romance in my parents' marriage is a little pill that yields a *huge* result; my dad was all too eager to take that pill.

There were other "little pills" I saw them take. For instance, my mom developed a loyalty to my dad that would rival battle armor in terms of protective quality. My dad honed his cooking skills so he could participate in their weekend ritual of jointly cooking a meaningful Saturday lunch. My mom learned to love the operational side of business to the point that she became a valued board member of my dad's ministry. My dad trained me from the time I was four or five years old to always be the one to open doors for my mom. I'd hop in the backseat of Dad's car, ready to go wherever we were headed, and within seconds, I'd see stink-eyes in the rearview mirror. Reflexively I'd double-check my seat belt, thinking, *What? What did I do?* and then it would dawn on me, a beam of bright recognition cutting through the thick, soupy fog: *Mom!* I'd jump out of the car, run around to the passenger side, open the door, and wave my open palm through the air, inviting my beloved mother to have a seat. What my dad was communicating to her all those times was that he valued her so much that he was going to teach their son to value her too, and to value *all* women.

On and on the list could go. They've faithfully tended to the little things because little things matter; in the end, they are a big, big deal. Just as those tiny muscle relaxers afforded me predictability, happiness, and health, sorting out the "little pills" of marriage can serve up the *very same positive results.*

As I say, I hadn't really noticed all this until I was asked to walk through the agony of divorce. But with fresh determination that I would not fail again, I soaked up all the helpful learning I could find. And when God graciously crossed my path with the wise and winsome Laura Cornett Thorne, I thought, *Here's my shot. I'm taking it. And I'm going to get this right.*

This isn't always easy, I know. It wasn't easy for my parents, certainly, and it proves to be an equal challenge for every couple willing to try. What I'm making the case for is that effort, though. We simply have to try.

The man who married Laura and me, Jim Burns, told us once that some marriages require a lot of work and some marriages require a little, but all marriages require *some.* There was

wisdom in that statement; it reminded me that if you want depth
and delight in the marriage relationship, you've got to do more
than coast. Today what that looks like for us is a whole lot of
maintenance.

Maintenance is a wonderful thing; it means you've achieved
some level of stability and now simply need to not screw it up. You
can't maintain something that never has been present, so Laura
and I have always viewed the maintenance efforts we apply to
our marriage as a good thing. To us, it is saying, "Let's keep the
momentum going that we've built." And so, we attend marriage
conferences and seminars. We listen to podcasts on having effective relationships. We read books together. We go on trips together
for the sole purpose of elbowing past busy schedules and the ever-
present demands of having kids and reconnecting as husband and
wife.

We also go to counseling, which is the maintenance in which
we're presently engaged. Over the next few weeks, Laura will log
fifteen hours with a counselor on her own; I'll do fifteen hours on
my own; and then, once we've both completed our individual work,
we'll do a few sessions together, as a couple. We're not doing this to
solve any real problems; we're doing it to keep real problems at bay.

A few months ago, Laura and I took Lincoln and Luci on a trip
to California with us, to visit family and friends. As is customary
when we are there, we made sure that at least one of our lunches
was spent at an In-N-Out burger joint. If you've never been to
In-N-Out, I should clarify that while the meal is as good as one
without utensils can be, this is not exactly a high-brow place. And
yet here was the scene on this most recent trip, as my family and I
left our local In-N-Out:

Me: Ahh. That was good.

Laura: It was. Honey, *thank you* for lunch today.

Me: [INSERT STUNNED SILENCE FOR THE EIGHTY-MIL-
LIONTH TIME IN MY MARRIAGE OVER THIS WOMAN'S KIND
AND GRACIOUS STYLE.]

Laura: Lincoln, tell Daddy thank you for lunch, please.
Wasn't lunch good today?

Lincoln: Thank you for lunch today, Daddy! I loved,
loved, loved my fries.

Me: [INSERT PUFFED-OUT CHEST AND OVERWHELMED
FEELINGS OF PRIDE.] You guys are the best.

Had Luci been of an age to communicate with understandable
words at that point, I'm sure Laura would have gotten her to say
thanks as well. Who *does* that, I ask you? I'll tell you who: *my wife.*

It's a little thing, yes—I'll grant you that. But it's a little thing
that makes me *melt.* Every man wants to be treated with respect,
and my wife sees to it I am.

On the flip side of the coin, I learned long ago that Laura loves
to receive cards from me, and also flowers from time to time. So,
it's not uncommon to find me standing in the greeting-card aisle
of our local grocery store, looking dense and confused I'm sure,
as I try to sort through all those thousands of cards. I painstak-
ingly stand there and carefully select ten or twelve cards—*different* cards, mind you . . . not just a dozen of the same one—and
then head back to my office with those cards in hand, where I sit
down at my computer, open up my calendar, and insert reminders for one week into the future, two weeks into the future, three
weeks into the future—all the way up to ten or twelve weeks into
the future, each of which reads, "card to Laura," for one reason

only: because Laura loves to receive cards. And what Laura loves, I love—or am committed to *learning* to love, at least.

Same goes for flowers. I know not all women enjoy a vase of freshly cut flowers around the house, but my wife does. Every once in a while, she'll drop a hint—something subtle, such as, "I need flowers"—and I know that either I stop on my way home from work and scratch the itch, or else in a few days' time I'll find a vase of beautiful roses on the coffee table that my wife had to purchase herself. I always feel like a shmuck when that happens, but what was I expecting? I'm grateful I'm married to a woman who *tells me what she needs* (another little thing that makes a big, big difference in our home), and also a woman who is fully capable of taking care of things herself, when her easily distractible husband drops the ball.

By way of contrast, there is a scene in the movie *The Breakup*, when after dinner one evening, the very irritated girlfriend asks the boyfriend who is sitting on the couch playing video games to help her with the dishes. He throws the gaming remote on the floor and heads toward the kitchen, saying, "Fine. I'll help you with the dishes," to which she says, "Oh, *come on*. No, see, that's not what I want," to which he says, "You just said that you want me to help you do the dishes," to which she says, "I want you to *want* to do the dishes."

I think I can speak for every man alive that we are never going to *want* to do the dishes. But in a healthy, life-giving relationship, what one partner always *will* want to do is please the other. The question that remains is, *what would be pleasing to them?*

In the strongest, happiest marriages I see, both partners are committed to answering that question, and then they are committed to doing those things.

I know couples who watch old movies together, or travel together, or join bowling clubs as man and wife. They practice speaking words of encouragement to each other, or they laugh easily with each other, or they learn to garden or speak Mandarin Chinese. They work to hold their tongue, or to offer a loving touch, or to settle matters quickly so anger never builds. They do the simple stuff of smiling, and holding hands, and taking walks, praying, and pouring end-of-day cups of hot tea. They persevere with the little things, because they've learned—often the hard way—that it's the little things that yield the biggest results.

finding your exceptional life

1. What "little things" do you tend to observe in marriages that seem to work?

2. When have you seen "little things" yield big results in the relationships you've known?

3. What character traits of Christ show up when we're faithful to tend to the little stuff of our marital worlds?

7

be who you are

Be who you are and say what you feel because those who
mind don't matter and those who matter don't mind.

—Dr. Seuss

y father and I may share a last name, but we're about as different as two men can be. My dad is highly organized, for
example, something I never will be accused of being. He loves
cataloguing information so passionately, in fact, that he nearly
majored in statistics in college and took on the role as his life's
work. I'd sooner poke out my eyes than become a statistician, but
for my dad the mere *mention* of numerical reasoning can keep him
fired up for hours on end.

When my dad started his ministry, Focus on the Family, he
quickly began receiving letters from radio listeners who wanted his

input on their parenting travails. So, because he figured a personal letter deserved a personal response, he'd sit down at his desk and write a letter back. He did this not for one or two listeners, but for them all. And he did this for more than two decades' time.

A lesser man would have smiled on his righteousness and called it a day, but no, no, not my dad. In addition to taking the time to *read* every letter and *respond personally* to every letter, he also decided to make a photocopy of both letter and reply. After twenty years, he had a fairly exhaustive set of archives on his hands—by then he'd logged his thoughts on every psychology-related topic imaginable.

It was then that a smart staffer at Focus said, "If we could digitize all that information, we could use it to reply to the letters we receive today and save Dr. Dobson a lot of time." The "letters" he was referring to numbered three-quarters of a million a month—*actual* letters, from *actual* listeners, containing *actual* pressing questions about how to get it right as parent and spouse. A mom from Paducah, Kentucky, would write, asking why despite her best efforts her four-year-old kept throwing temper tantrums and why he still insisted on sucking his thumb. A couple from White Plains, New York, wanted to know how to deal with the defiance of a seven-year-old daughter who now refused to go to school. A grandfather from Los Angeles would reach out, explaining he needed help with his adult son, who no longer had any use for God.

Thanks to innovations in technology at the time, staff members could type in key words—"thumb-sucking," "strong-willed," "spiritual apathy," and the like—and chunks of content would then appear on-screen, which they could cut and paste into a letter of response. Sure, while it wasn't actually my dad responding, it was *his content* responding, each and every time. And countless millions of families I think would agree that this ingenious system helped improve parenting and save sanity across the land.

All this, because my dad has been, is, and always will be organized.

Those hard-copy letters and responses still occupy a fair amount of space in my father's massive filing system, which is located in his office at our studio, a place so laden with paper it would rival the Library of Congress for number of trees killed so that it can be in existence. In addition to ministry correspondence, my dad has kept every "note to self" he's ever written—late-night ideas for his radio broadcast, firsthand stories that would make good book illustrations, magazine articles with his margin-scribbled observations and critiques. If he has thought it, he has written it down; and if he has written it down, he has filed it away for future use. What's more, if you were to say, "Hey, Doc, what are your thoughts on the whole climate-change thing?" he could actually *lead you to the appropriate file.* More than five decades' worth of introspection, right at his fingertips.

It's impressive. It's invaluable. And it's a reality I'll never know.

My office is more grunge-art exhibit meets hyperactive pack rat, which for a guy with severe ADHD like me is an absolute dream. For my dad? Not so much. There are days when the floor of my office is carpeted with so many in-process food items, strewn-about copies of *Garden and Gun* magazine, dusty stacks of soon-to-be-read books, upside-down skateboards, and piles of snaked cords that go to who-knows-which piece of electronic gear that my father will not come in. I even have a hard time coming in under those circumstances, and I created this madness myself. If I do choose to enter, I groan, "Why can't I be more like my dad?"

Then there is schooling. Between my dad and me, one of us dutifully went to college, served in the Army, graduated from a challenging Ph.D. program, and thrived in each evolution of his career—educator, counselor, researcher, private-practice psychologist, crusader for all-things family . . . while the other dutifully went to college but got kicked out for poor grades, strived for a job in construction or as the president of the United States but would reach neither goal in the end, eventually went back to college and actually did okay, circuitously dabbled in rock music, youth ministry, surfing, professional fighting, and pretty much proved himself a full wanderer when it was all said and done.

I'll let you guess who is who.

I look back now and see that while my dad's meteoric rise to the top echelon of Christian influencers in this country didn't seem to impact him in any meaningful way, it did in fact impact me. I didn't especially like being famous—or at least the son of someone who was—and so I did a lot of running—from my roots, from my family, from my name.

When I was a senior in high school and it was time for me to think about going to college, I remember bucking the entire idea. My dad and I would have long talks about this issue—more the case, he would have long talks, while I would be asked to listen—but I never became convinced that this was the path for me. Eventually I'd be persuaded to go because my best friend had also been persuaded, thanks to my highly persuasive dad.

Jonah and I went from being carefree California skateboarders to buttoned-up collegiates who were required to wear sports coats in the school cafeteria on the Sabbath each week. We had enrolled in a school ninety minutes south of Chicago and on a near-daily basis would survey the farmland surrounding us and think, *What on earth have we done?*

It snowed in May our first year there. *Dear Lord, save us from this place.*

I quickly realized that being in *this* town with *my* last name was a recipe for disaster from the start. In Illinois at the time, it was Jesus Christ and James Dobson, and a hot, bright spotlight seemed to follow me wherever I'd go. I wasn't used to this type of attention, and I'd prove to handle it less than well. But honestly, we *all* tend to fail when people's expectations of us are unreasonably grand.

I once heard that you should never digitally alter a photo of yourself to make yourself look better, because when people actually see you in person, they'll be disappointed. Hype is a tough thing to live up to, and that's exactly what followed me to school: *hype.* And yet, for my father, things were vastly different. Perhaps because he had more maturity under his belt, or a deeper, more dependable walk with Christ, he kept on being himself, even as the spotlight seared us all.

After becoming an adult I'd often be asked if I struggled with my identity during my growing-up years because I was adopted. My friend Doug was with me once when the question came my way, and before I could offer a pat answer, he interjected, "I think Ryan struggled so much with being a Dobson that it made all other issues pale in comparison."

Doug was absolutely correct.

I haven't done much in my life out of sheer spite, but the first tattoo I bought myself I'm pretty sure was borne of spite. Sort of a, "Ha! Take that! A Dobson with *ink* for a change."

It's the only tattoo I have that I hate. I should have never gotten it done. But even then, my dad didn't judge me. There were a few audible groans, as I distinctly recall, but judgment and shame? Not a lick. His one caution to me was this: "You are a follower of Christ, Ryan, which means He has important work for you to do. I'd hate to see you unnecessarily limit your ministry because of something as silly as a tattoo."

It would be the first of a thousand side comments regarding my clothing, my piercings, and my hair. I'd show up at my parents' house wearing a Mexican poncho and jeans, to which my father would slowly shake his head—code for, "Have you seen how sloppy you look?"

I'd dye my hair green or come home with black gauges (large earrings) in both ears or add yet another tattoo, and I'd get that same slow head-shake: *Ryan, Ryan, Ryan.*

Eventually, I'd say, "Dad, it's okay—it is. I don't need for you to understand." And then we'd move on to more consequential things—politics and discipleship and fighting the really good fights.

It took a big man to acquiesce on these fronts—I can see that plainly now. My father was weaned on *Dress for Success* and still today is rarely found without shirtsleeves and slacks—even if he's just hanging out at home. To be handed a son—an *only* son—who has little use for obligation or propriety must at some level make him cringe. And yet that's not the expression I get. Far from it: the look on his face I've seen most every day of my life is one of acceptance and appreciation and joy. It's the expression of a guy who loves me just as I am—quirkiness, different-from-him-ness, and all.

But given that I was quirky, that I was totally different from my dad, what did that mean for me? It takes a long time to get to know ourselves, doesn't it; we can't "be who we are" until we *first know who we are.*

I had an aha moment when I was seventeen years old. It centered on the realization that although I had no desire to be a clone of my father, there were aspects of his life I did crave. I wanted his confidence, for example, and his bent toward compassion. I wanted his sense of justice, and also his way with words. I wanted to be a man of my convictions, and I wanted to be a good husband, a good dad to my kids. I couldn't have predicted how my dreams would come true in this regard, back when I was a know-it-all teen with the world by its tail. But I'm grateful for the path God led me down; those simple steps have saved my life.

In 1986, I was sixteen years old, and that was the year my parents mentioned in passing that the Summit, a local ministry, would be hosting a two-week summer program on biblical worldview they thought I might like. "It's sort of like summer school, but you'll like it," they said. "Do you think you might want to go?"

Camp. With classes. My parents needed new PR.

"No," I said, by way of reply. "But thank you for thinking of me."

The following year, my parents came around again. "You know that 'camp' we mentioned to you last year?" they asked. "Tell you what. You agree to go, and that car of yours will *still be yours* upon your return back home."

I got the message, loud and clear.

It probably goes without saying that I showed up resentful, haughty, and mad at Camp with Classes, as I began lovingly calling it. I was too old for camp and too smart for classes, and I knew this would be a waste of my time. That is, until I knew that it absolutely wasn't.

Camp with Classes, day one: wake up at 6:00 a.m., clean my room and make my bed, head to the dining hall, eat, be in my seat ready to learn promptly by 8:00 a.m., prepared to have our minds absolutely blown. These people meant *business*. Camp organizers had flown in the best minds in Christian scholarship to teach us peons about big-ticket subjects such Christology and ecclesiology, history and sociology, psychology and anthropology, and other -ologies of which I'd never heard. I realized within three hours of my little two-week experience that my safe, secure world was being totally rocked. On day three, we were made to watch Francis Schaeffer's series *How Should We Then Live*, and I actually suffered a headache, my brain was working so hard.

Growing up in church, I learned the pat answers to keep nay-sayers at bay. Here, they didn't teach me answers; they taught me *how to think*. It would be a distinction with monumental consequences for me—I was finally discovering who I was.

The band Alice in Chains has an instrumental dirge from their 1994 album *Jar of Flies* called "Whale and Wasp," and about twenty seconds before the song ends, there's this crazy dissonance that emerges, totally unexpected and wildly captivating. This is how my camp experience was for me—melodic notes bumping into a tall brick wall, a necessary disruption of all that I knew to be true. Life's defining moments always happen that way; we're skating along with blades in one set of grooves until we're thrown off-balance by something terrifying or wonderful or both and then must capture our center of gravity all over again.

My parents said I came home from camp a different person. My take on it looking back is a shade different: I came home from camp *a person*. For the first time in my young life, I was becoming me—distinctly, definitely (maybe defiantly) me. I think this had been my dad's goal all along. He wasn't going to spend his parenting chits on hair color or tattoos or clothes; no, he would save those for one key thing: *what did I make of the truth?*

He was determined to know truth for himself, to enjoy living in light of that truth, and then to expose me to that bright light. He then was committed to standing back and watching what I did with it—would it arrest me? change me? penetrate the tall walls I'd built?

This is the gift my dad gave me: he provided enough rope for me either to hang myself, or else to knot myself to an anchor that would weather every one of life's storms. Of course that anchor is Jesus, and wisely, I chose that route.

Nearly eight years ago, my dad was walking on stage to speak at an event in Nashville, when he received an urgent call. When he travels, he has security go with him, and it was one of them who'd answered his phone. "Yes?" he said, "This is Joe, for Dr. Dobson. May I ask who is calling please?"

It was me on the other end. "Joe, it's Ryan. Put my dad on!" I said excitedly. "Now, now! Put him on!"

"Ryan, he's going on stage right this minute. He's already been introduced."

"I know, I know," I said, "but you've got to get him. He will definitely want to hear this."

I could tell I was causing all sorts of issues for my dad and his team, but honestly, I didn't care. Within seconds, I heard my dad's voice on the line, saying, "Hello? Hello? Who's calling, please?"

Joe had simply thrust the phone toward my father's ear, saying, "Sir, you've got to take this call . . ."

"Dad!" I said. "Listen . . . listen! Can you hear that? Can you hear that, Dad?"

My father's first grandchild was being born in that moment, and the baby's wailing only increased in sound.

"What's going on?" my dad said, panicked. "Ryan? Ryan, are you there?"

"Dad, *listen*," I implored him again. "Stop talking for a second . . . can you hear that sound?"

As my dad settled into the sounds from the other end of the line, revelation finally eclipsed the confusion he'd felt. "I'm a grandpa!" I heard him shout into the receiver. "My grandson! He's being born!"

We had so hoped my parents would be present when Laura went into labor, but this was a close second for sure. My dad and I shared a few quick seconds of heartfelt laughter and tears, and then I knew he had to go. People who were in attendance at that talk would later tell me that he opened his remarks by bounding onto the stage, puffing out his chest, and proclaiming, "Ladies and gentlemen, exactly sixty seconds ago, I became a grandfather for the very first time," to which the crowd unabashedly roared and cheered.

I look at Lincoln still today—he's seven, going on eight—and I think, *You don't fully know it yet, but you are ridiculously blessed. To have God put you in this lineage, in a family that will love you this well . . . you're more blessed than you know.*

I wonder what his life's trajectory will be—the places he'll go, the decisions he'll make, the person he will someday become— and I praise God that I was raised by a dad who majors in the majors, and who lets the minors unfold as they may. Lincoln has high highs and low lows and is gutsy and artistic and smart—in a thousand ways he is just like me, but in thousands more, he's his own man. He loves team sports, for instance, which is a little amusing to his anti-team-sports dad. I've always gravitated toward skating, surfing, wrestling, fighting—things you can compete in on your own—but since my son is into baseball, I now am into baseball. I'm into baseball because I'm into *him*. It's a lesson I learned from my dad: make big deals of the big deals, and let the little deals—hair color, clothing choices, sports preferences—fall where they may.

As it relates to my kids—Lincoln and little Luci too—I've decided that wherever they go and whatever they do, however they live and whomever they love, I will do my level best to keep my heart and my arms wide open, always eager to welcome in these two I totally adore.

finding your exceptional life

1. Have you ever found yourself working hard to fit into someone else's framework of who you should be, what you should wear, how you should act, and so forth? What were the circumstances that led to your conformity?

2. When do you find it most difficult to simply "be who you are"?

3. There's an axiom that says, "Be who you are; everyone else is taken." What natural strengths, talents, abilities, passions, and insights do you (and only you!) bring to the world around you? Why is it important that you bring your best self constantly to bear?

The day I was adopted and became a Dobson.

Dad and me at the age of two.

Me and my paternal grandfather "Gee Gee."

My maternal
grandfather "Grandpa
Joe" and me.

Starting
trouble early.

My sister
Danae and
I (serious
80s).

This is my second "real" skateboard at age ten.

Dad and me fishing in Canada at the age of thirteen.

Danae and I at my Jr. High graduation.

Dad and me walking in London, age sixteen.

Pheasant hunting with my dad, age twenty-four.

My first date with Laura (she's a little afraid of pelicans).

Engagement
party with
Laura.

Our wedding day.

Wedding day with
Laura and her
parents, Steve and
Linda.

Wedding photos by Ira Lippke Studios

Walking through the tunnel of surfboards.

Cutting the
cake with
custom surfing
bride and
groom toppers.

We left California
for the snow in
Colorado!

Wedding photos by Ira Lippke Studios

My sweet
wife Laura.

Laura in
Jackson
Hole,
Wyoming,
in the fall.

Laura and I
with my
parents.

My dad and I in the snow.

Rafting with the guys at "Man Camp."

Feeding kangaroos with Linc.

My parents and Lincoln.

Lincoln in Hawaii.

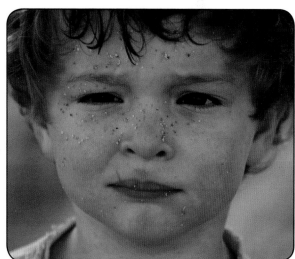

Linc on the beach.

Me and Lincoln.

Mom and
Lincoln.

Lincoln
fishing
with
Grampa
Steve.

Dad and I at
Harvest.

Family photo before
Luci was born.

Lincoln
and I
LOVE
fishing.

Linc
with his
grandpas.

Sledding
with Linc
(the GoPro
footage is
epic!).

Linc and I
feeding the
chickens.

Linc swinging for the stars.

Newborn
Luci Primrose
Dobson.

Laura and Baby Lu.

Can you feel the love?

The sweetest
baby ever.

Linc and Lu
adore each
other.

Grampa
Steve and
the kids.

Dobsons at Halloween (Lumberjacks, Luke and a baby zebra).

Someone got teeth.

Hiking with my littlest love.

Underwater Lincoln.

Lu loves the
pool too.

Laura took this
shot of us dancing
to Mumford and
Sons (Lu's fav).

My babes.

8

whatever it takes

I don't remember who said this, but there really
are places in the heart you don't even know exist
until you love a child.

—ANNE LAMOTT

My dad is not a man governed by fear, but there was a time in his life when a pervasive fear haunted him night and day. It was just after my adoption, after he and my mom had brought me home at six weeks old, and simultaneously, my father's ministry was taking off and his book sales were going through the roof. His publisher had asked him to carve out time to do book signings in various cities, and so for several years in a row, my dad spent a portion of his time at churches and convention centers and bookstores, seated behind a table, signing strangers' copies of his books.

He wouldn't disclose this to me until I was a grown man myself, but evidently during those book signings, he was racked by the fear of my birth mother approaching the table where he sat, demanding to take back her little boy. "The only thing I knew to do," he told me, "was to come up with a plan."

And so he had. If someone approached my father with the intent of taking me away, he decided, he was going to slip away, rush home, grab a few necessities—including his wife, his daughter, and me—and race to the airport. From there, the four of us were going to fly to New Zealand, relocating there immediately, overnight. "There was no chance I would ever, ever, ever let you go," he said.

He said "ever" three times, just like that; I remember each and every one.

"I would have given up my practice, my career, my ministry, and even my country, Ryan, if it meant being able to be with you. Letting you go just wasn't an option," he said. "I was willing to do *whatever it took* to stay connected to you."

This wasn't legalities or logistics to him; this was a matter of love. We pursue that which we care about. My dad was determined to show me he cared.

My father revealed those early fears to me when I was thirty years old. At the time, I was between marriages, between jobs, between residences, between *lives* really, and was shot through with deep-seated pain. I was lonely and desperate and unsettled and scared . . . and then along came my dad with those words:

"Letting you go just wasn't an option, Ryan. I'd have done anything to be with you."

My soul perked up for the first time that year. I was *loved*. I was *seen*. I was worthy of being pursued. It had been this way my entire life, and it was true for me still that day.

In what would prove a compelling study in contrast, a few weeks after my dad and I had that talk, a family I knew asked if I'd help them out. The parents had to go on a business trip, and their three kids would be home alone. "We'd feel better if there were an adult in the house," they said, "to take care of meals and daily life." I was in youth ministry back then and was used to being around junior- and senior-high kids. They figured it was a natural fit.

Plus, they'd said, since their youngest son was only thirteen at the time, they wanted to make sure he was tended to. The mom mentioned in passing that Mark, the son, had a "little girlfriend" and that it was fine if the two of them wanted to hang out at the house, as long as I kept a close eye on things.

The first day of my house-sitting stint, I met Mark outside his junior high and, per his request, then drove to his girlfriend's house to pick her up. Mark and I pulled up to the house and noticed his girlfriend's father in the front yard, dressed in full "dad" regalia: a T-shirt and shorts with sandals . . . and black socks pulled up to his calves. He looked up from the plants he was watering and gave us a subtle wave.

A few minutes later, Mark's girlfriend emerged, and my jaw nearly hit the floorboard. The outfit she'd chosen for this little after-school date revealed a mile of belly and eight miles of leg. I looked over at Mark, who reflexively emitted a groan as he took her in. I looked back at the girl and then at the girl's father, fully expecting a fight of biblical proportions to break out as soon as the father saw the daughter's attire. *He's going to lose his mind!* I thought. *And then he's going to look at me—a thirty-year-old man, for crying out loud—and think this whole thing is somehow my fault.*

I envisioned the dad having me thrown in jail for causing delinquency in his little girl. "She can't get in my truck dressed like that!" I shouted at Mark, who was now slinking down in his seat. "Her father will have me killed!"

The scene unfolded in slow motion, as the girlfriend came into her father's line of sight. She walked by him as she made her way to my truck, and I held my breath in anticipation of an all-out daddy/daughter war.

"Bye, Daddy," she said breezily, as she slipped into the truck, through the passenger door Mark had opened for her.

"See ya," her father said in response, barely looking up from his watering hose.

That's it? I thought incredulously. *But didn't he see what she has on?*

I've never been more concerned about avoiding driving infractions as I was during that brief trip back to Mark's house. Furthermore, for the entire three miles, I had my body plastered to the driver-side door, staying as far away as possible from the scantily clad thirteen-year-old to my right. Mark, who was a good kid trying to go God's way in his life, was plastered to the passenger-side door, equally fearful that this cute young girl between us would somehow cause him to sin, and there in the middle sat the girlfriend, chattering nonstop without a care in the world.

A few minutes later, blissfully, we arrived at Mark's house. I couldn't disembark quickly enough. Once inside and able to breathe normally again, I spotted the girlfriend heading for the half-bath, which was just inside the front door. Over her shoulder was slung a tiny backpack that looked like it could fit perhaps three M&Ms inside, but after a few moments passed, she re-emerged from the bathroom wearing jeans and a long-sleeved tee. I looked at her and then looked at Mark, whose expression was as perplexed as my own. *What in the world?* we said silently to each other. *What was that about?*

That Wednesday night I showed up at my church's youth-group meeting, where I led the group of high-school kids. I gathered a few of the girls around me, laid out the entire scenario, just as it had occurred—the shockingly inappropriate outfit, followed by the shockingly fast wardrobe change—and then asked, "Can you help me understand her thinking here?"

They all had been nodding bobbleheads the entire time, offering verbal reinforcements as I told my tale—"Mm-hmmm. Yeah. Uh-huh. Right, right, right."—and then summed up the issue with a penetrating assessment. "It makes perfect sense," one of the young women said, on behalf of her peers standing there. "The girl was just seeing if her dad loves her or not. The fact that she reached your truck without a word from her dad told her all she needed to know."

The irony was thick: my dad had just revealed to me that he would have moved heaven and earth, he would have forsaken career and country, in order to protect his beloved child, and yet here was a girl all but begging for care—care that she'd never receive. By her actions she demanded her father fight for her heart, and yet there he stood, oblivious and lame. She was screaming, "Love me! See me! Pursue me, please! Show me that you care." And yet the flower beds would get more of his attention that day, as she skipped off half-naked with two men.

I saw a bumper sticker once that read, "Guns don't kill people. Dads with daughters kill people." I'm not pro-murder, you understand. But I am very much pro-pursuit. And I think every little girl alive today would give anything to have a big, strong daddy make sure she is treated well. Little girls want dads who say, "Sweetheart, when you're old enough for boys to start coming by the house, I want you to know that I will be standing there on the front porch polishing my guns as they arrive. And I'm going to have dogs. *Mean* dogs. And a big tattoo across my neck that says, 'I kill boys.'"

Our kids—our daughters and also our sons—want parents who say, "I love you. I see you. And even if I have to travel to the ends of the earth, I'm going to pursue you with everything I've got."

Yes, they'll roll their eyes and feign disgust and tell us we're being overprotective crazy people for drawing boundary lines that in their view are ridiculously tight, but you know what they'll be thinking, even as they spout out those words? They'll think, *I've got parents who will do whatever it takes to prove to me they care.*

It was then, after that incident with Mark and his girlfriend, that I made a vow to myself, that if and when God blessed me with children of my own, I'd be a whatever-it-takes kind of dad.

When Lincoln was born nearly eight years ago, a protective side of me I didn't know existed began to rise to the surface and ooze out all over my son. Early on, a buddy of mine even accused me of overprotection: "What, are you going to put him in a bubble his whole life?" to which I smiled and said, "Yeah! For a while, anyway. And you want to know why? I'm the only dad he's got!"

There's a plain fact about parenting that despite our culture's best efforts at thwarting remains uncomfortably true: When you and I sign on to become moms and dads, we're agreeing to steward *another person's soul.* We are that kid's primary shot at growing up safe and strong and spiritually pointed toward God—a *huge* task, to be sure. Look around and you'll see that our kids are being "marketed to" at younger and younger ages. Futurist Faith Popcorn predicts that in the next millennium "we're going to see health clubs for kids, kids as experts on things like the Internet, and new businesses like Kinko's for Kids, to provide professional-quality project presentations."[4]

Maybe there's nothing wrong with trends such as these, but maybe there is. Maybe there really is a price to pay when we treat children not as children but, as Kay Hymowitz says, "as small adults."

My kids, Lincoln and Luci, are *not* small adults. They are *kids.* And kids need to be lovingly, carefully trained up, in order to effectively navigate life. They need to be protected at all costs—to the ends of the earth, if you will. We shelter them now so that we can help them soar later.

The summer before my freshman year of high school, my parents sat me down and struck a deal. I would go to a Christian school that year in exchange for veto rights my sophomore year. They were convinced that if I'd just give Christian high school a chance, I'd love it as much as they loved it themselves. In fact, I was already over my Christian-education quota, given that if you count kindergarten I'd put in *nine long years* by that point. But parents have a lot of leverage in these arrangements, and even an immature thirteen-year-old knows the score. I liked having food to eat, for instance, as well as clothes to wear. I liked the idea of having a car to drive once I was licensed, and getting birthday and Christmas presents each year. I gathered that this arrangement was more demand than friendly deal: Despite the fact that I didn't see myself as a Christian school sort of kid, my freshman year indeed would be spent attending Christian school.

I wasn't very happy about it. At the end of the first quarter of my freshman year, my dad and I left for a three-day pheasant-hunting trip in South Dakota. It was a memory-making trip, not so much because of the hunting, which truly was fantastic, but because of a single conversation my father and I had. That talk left such an impression on me that still today, some thirty years later, I could take you right to the room where it occurred.

Partway through our trip, my dad sat down next to me and asked how school was going. He knew full well how it was going, but I think he wanted to give me a chance to say it here, in person, face to face, just him and me.

Never one to soften blows, I said plainly, "I hate it."

It wasn't that I hated being in a Christian school; it's that I hated being a *Dobson* in a Christian school. There were fewer than fifty kids in the entire freshman class, which meant everyone knew who I was. I was tired of being known.

In response, I expected my dad to reiterate the terms of the deal we'd made—that I would attend the Christian school for my *entire* freshman year before making any decisions—and then remind me that we still had three quarters to go. But that's not at all what he did. Instead, he studied my face for a moment. He nodded his head subtly, as though he were understanding something for the first time. He said, "Hang on a second, okay?" And then he did something I'll never forget. He picked up a nearby phone from its cradle, he dialed his assistant back in California, and he said these words: "I want Ryan taken off the roster at his school and enrolled at Arcadia High by the time we return. And I know it's asking a lot, but I'd like his only responsibility to be cleaning out his locker at his old school and showing up at his new school the following day."

And just like that, I became an Arcadia High School Apache. I was done with Christian school.

His swift actions that day told me all I needed to know. This man *cared for my heart*. What's more, he saw me as one who was making my way from adolescence to adulthood, and doing not too bad of a job. Sure, my dad's decision to let me transfer to public school had to have been frightening—for him and also for my mom. My dad was a clinical psychologist who understood the dangers I'd face. He knew how easily I might be swept up in the current of a culture that didn't have my best interest at heart. And yet he also knew *me*. He knew that in that situation I needed to have my perspective considered, that I needed to be heard by him. He wasn't blindly acquiescing here; he was taking a calculated risk. I was a good kid with a good heart who made good decisions most of the time. The trust he was placing in me in that moment would forever change how I viewed my dad. He knew when to hold me tight, and when to let me go.

He knew the difference between a child and a son becoming an adult. I'm a better man as a result.

finding your exceptional life

1. Did you feel pursued and protected by your parents during growing-up years? How has the reality of that upbringing impacted the person you are today?

2. In what ways have you seen boundaries—even strict ones—serve you and your family well?

3. What would being a "whatever-it-takes" parent look like in the context of your role today? What skills or character traits would you require more of?

9

it's always new

There is no greater risk than matrimony.
But there is nothing happier than a happy marriage.
—Benjamin Disraeli

A few weeks before Laura and I were married, I was having a conversation with my dad about how to thrive as a couple, about the time-tested practices that for almost fifty years and counting had made my parents' marriage great. He mentioned several things I'd heard him preach to couples all my life—be intentional about creating healthy experiences that bond you to your mate, keep lines of communication open, don't go to bed angry but instead keep short accounts, and the like—and then he chuckled and said this: "You'll get a kick out of this. Just yesterday I woke up before your mom did, I rolled over in bed and looked at her, and I had the funniest thought run through my mind. I thought, *Who are you?*"

My dad continued. "Every married person asks that question of his or her spouse," he said, "but in a flash of insight, I realized that one of the keys to a happy marriage is asking it out of fascination, not frustration. We either ask, 'Who *are* you?'—as in, how on earth did I get here, married to someone as passive and pathetic as you?—or we ask, 'Who are *you*?'—as in, I bet I'm going to learn something about you today I never knew before, and I'm preparing myself in advance to like that new thing I find."

He went on to say that although he had been married to my mom for decades and decades and knew her better than anyone else on Planet Earth, *still* he doesn't know who she is. "And I think that's exactly the way God intended it," he said. "He made man, and He made woman, and He made the two of them incredibly distinct. We are fearfully made. We are *frighteningly* different. And I think God gets a kick out of that."

Then my father said this: "The thing about a happy marriage, Ryan, is that both partners relish the mystery of each other, instead of assuming they know all there is to know. They realize that if they will treasure the process of continuing to discover their spouse, their marriage will always be brand new."

This was really good advice, advice I immediately took to heart. I thought about the first time I met Laura—it was on a blind date—and within six minutes was intrigued. It was 100 percent, "Who are *you*?"

All fascination.

All magnetism.

All determination to sort her out.

I could see that what my dad was saying was, "Don't let that fascination die, Ryan. Don't let fascination devolve into frustration. Instead, fight to keep the element of surprise alive."

There was substance to my dad's perspective that day; in fact, the element of surprise was the first important building block of my parents' lifelong love affair.

During the days when my parents were attending school at Pasadena College, nearby Long Beach boasted a waterfront boardwalk featuring The Pike amusement park. The biggest draw there was a giant roller coaster positioned over the ocean called the Cyclone Racer, and between 1930 and 1968, more than thirty million people had the thrill of boarding that ride. One of those people was my mom, despite her vehement insistence against it.

It was my parents' third date and my father's idea: "Let's go to the boardwalk and ride the Cyclone!" to which my mother said, "Not a chance."

My mom didn't "do" roller coasters.

And my dad didn't take no for an answer.

He eventually goaded her into boarding the ride, and she gripped the safety bar so tightly for those two minutes that when she stepped back onto the platform when it was over, her fingers had frozen themselves into little fists. Through the crush of people they made their way back down to the boardwalk, and just as my dad was about to say, "That was *fun*, wasn't it?" my mom collapsed, fainting right there on the spot.

My dad always has been good in a crisis, but this one left him totally shocked. He barely even knows this woman, and now, *look*, he's caused her to faint.

"Shirley?" he shouted at my mom, who was lying flat on the slatted ground. "Shirley, can you hear me? Are you okay?"

A crowd was beginning to gather, as my dad crouched down and hovered over my mom. "Shirley? Shirley! Can you hear me?" He felt indicted, as though all these onlookers somehow knew he had forced this poor, pitiful young woman to do something she hadn't wanted to do.

He began to check her vital signs—heart rate fine, pulse fine, breathing normal, no fever as far as he could tell—and was patting her hand, willing her to wake up, to please, please open her eyes, when he peered into my mother's face and detected there on her lips a mischievous grin.

Yep. That's my mom for you. She had faked the entire thing.

Surprising, wouldn't you say? In that moment my dad knew that there were mysteries to this feisty woman he could spend a lifetime trying to solve.

He wanted in on that deal.

Well, Laura and I did get married, beginning a lifelong love affair of our own, and while I was terribly fascinated with her from the moment I met her, that fascination soon would be challenged. "Soon," as in two days into our wedded bliss.

We had traveled to a remote island for our honeymoon, thanks to a friend's generous offer to let us come stay in a hotel he owned in the vicinity, and we were ready for eleven days of total relaxation—sleeping in, surfing, eating great seafood, taking long walks on the beach. I had done a ton of online research leading up to our trip, chasing down information specifically on the best eateries and the best places to surf. Laura began surfing at age seven and had caught waves all over the world—in Morocco and France, in Japan and Australia, and, on a daily basis, in her home state of California. She's a *great* surfer, and I wanted her to be impressed.

One of the interesting tidbits I'd picked up from my research about this little island advised that we not surf during a certain block of the day while we were there, because this is when the locals surfed, and they weren't too keen on sharing their waves. *No problem,* I thought. I tucked away the information, determined to work around that schedule once we'd arrived and thus keep the natives happy and calm.

But Laura would have different ideas.

The first morning we woke up in our little bungalow, we had to pinch ourselves: Were we really here? Really *married*? Life couldn't get better than this. I looked at my new wife—how I ever won the affections of a woman this beautiful and smart, I didn't know—and shook my head in grateful disbelief. It was going to be a great day. It was going to be a great life.

I began to lay out my plans for the day—finding some breakfast, strolling around the tiny town, surfing later in the afternoon—when Laura interrupted and said, "Why don't we just go surfing now?"

I explained to her exactly why we couldn't surf now and then restated my plan.

"That's the dumbest thing I've ever heard," she said plainly. "I've surfed all over the world, and I've never once run into a problem with locals. Let's go for it!"

I explained to her yet again why we couldn't just "go for it," using phrases such as "because I value my life" and "because I

don't want to die on my honeymoon," to which she waved a dis-
missive hand through the air and said, "Ridiculous. Let's go!"

I stared at this beautiful, smart woman whom I'd ever so
recently married and thought, *Who are you?*

I'd done all the research.

I'd crafted a good plan.

Plus, I was the *husband*, for crying out loud.

Frankly, I wasn't all that fascinated right then. And "frus-
trated" would be a generous slant.

Looking back, it's a little embarrassing, the way I reacted to
my new wife. I tried to power up with her, which made her try
to power up with me, and the whole thing blew up in our face. It
would be our first real fight, and it would be a big one. I consider
my dad—the guy who still today, after walking through more
than half a century with my mom—can choose fascination over
frustration—and I think, *What, I couldn't give a little ground in my
own marriage on day two?*

Interestingly, after that whopper of a fight, Laura and I did go
surf. Right then. During mid-morning hours, while the locals were
vying for waves. And within ten minutes of the little boat taking
us out to the reef, every last fear of mine was validated in spades.
Ten locals were already surfing there, lots of them missing their
teeth; you don't surf these twenty-foot waves this close to a reef
without crashing and burning a few times. I surveyed one of them
in particular, who had melon-baller scoops of flesh missing from
his upper back and realized these were real-deal surfers who could
absolutely eat me for lunch. I can hold my own on a longboard,
but I'm five-ten, one hundred and seventy soaking wet. These guys
were Goliath; I was a shepherd boy.

As soon as we reached our drop-off point, Laura began paddling out in her carefree style, shouting, "Hi!" to each local she passed. She was cute and outgoing and disarming and blonde, while I was simply very vulnerable and now very alone.

I looked on as my wife took an overhead barrel wave and proceeded to do five big turns, and then I watched as ten local jaws dropped. Turning to face them, I said simply, by way of explanation, probably with a stupefied grin of relief, "She's good."

The missing-flesh man paddled over to me, and I was just sure my minutes were numbered. Approaching, he looked me over. "You want some weed?" he asked in a heavily accented voice. I declined, to which he said, "Cocaine?" Again, I declined, to which he said, "Ice?"

I later learned that ice was an island form of crystal meth, so I'm glad I declined that too.

His last question for me was, "Are you a cop?"

"No," I said, "I'm a pastor."

He looked perplexed. "Pastor?" he asked.

"Yeah," I said, putting the palms of my hands together at chest level. "You know . . . prayer?" I then pointed skyward. "God?"

"Ah!" he said. "Pastor! Yeah, yeah. *Pastor.*" He then began to shout to his buddies in his native tongue. What it sounded like to me was, "Ooben glimitch bleegon *pastor!*"

They all cheered and began waving at me. "Hi, pastor!" they said, now all smiles and sunshine.

"Hey," I said, relieved I was still alive.

Laura was still out catching waves, footloose and fancy-free, as my blood pressure finally returned to normal.

We still had nine more days on the island, and everywhere we went, we'd see those same guys, and each time, they'd exuberantly shout, "Pastor! Hi, Pastor! Hi Pastor Girl!"

And each time I would think, *I'm so happy I married Pastor Girl.*

I've been seeing a counselor named Betty for many years, and recently she asked, "Ryan, what would you say is the greatest contribution your parents have made to your life?"

My answer came to me in a flash. "A happy marriage," I said. "A marriage that is just as strong today as it was half a century ago."

It's the truth: what gets a lot of press is the damage that a bad marriage does to a kid, but there's a fantastic flip-side to that coin. You can't *imagine* the benefits to your children when your marriage is healthy and strong.

In the early 1980s, my parents went to a marriage conference that was popular back then, not so much because their own marriage needed help, but because, according to my dad, it would make for good research for his ministry. Even though he had shifted gears to become a radio talk-show host, he was and always will be a clinical psychologist at heart. He wanted to people-watch—that's what this came down to—and he would tell me years later that his favorite observation from the weekend was seeing the very same couples who had arrived and found seats and sat angled away from each other were, after three days of input and encouragement, now leaning in. By the third day of the conference they were curled into each other like the swirls of a snail shell, sharing knowing glances, gentle laughs, and easy smiles.

"They quit focusing on the old, and started drawing out the new," he'd say. This deeply moved my dad.

It was during that same weekend, inspired by the conference talks, that my dad sat down at the little desk in my parents' hotel room and penned that lengthy letter to my mom—still today, I can't read it without tearing up. My parents' married life hasn't always been easy, but I know it has always been good. It's been good because they have *made* it good; they have chosen to make it good. Through the toddler years and "new business venture" years and lean years and fat years alike, they have chosen to make it good. Through surgeries and health scares and the loss of loved ones and more, they have chosen to make it good. Through their twenties and thirties and forties and fifties and sixties and yes, even now, *they have chosen to make it good.*

This is highly instructive to me.

I thought about that letter a few months into my marriage to Laura, back when we were living in our first apartment, a tiny set of square rooms in the heart of San Clemente. We'd had an argument—about what, I can't recall—and I'd stormed out of the bedroom and into the living room, which was less dramatic than I'd intended, given the living room was only ten feet away. I think I may have slammed the bedroom door behind me, which would have added a little flair, but soon after I reached the living room, my anger screeched to a halt. The reason was simple: I'd caught sight of a picture, framed there on the entertainment center that was way too big for the room. The picture was of Laura, and she was wearing her wedding dress. She was seated on a daybed made in Bali, leaning back on her elbows, boasting a tender smile. Her dress was strapless, and she was gorgeous. I fell in love all over again.

The train of thought that occurred to me, even on the heels of a fuming fit, was, *"I'm going to grow old with that woman. I'm going to someday be a wrinkly old man, and that incredible person is going to be wiping drool from my mouth. We're going to sit next to each other in little rocking chairs, reminiscing about this exact teeny-tiny apartment. We're going to watch our kids have kids themselves and then laugh as they make the same mistakes we did. We're going to rack up all this life together, and then we're going to shake our heads in amazement over the good things God has done. And yet I'm fighting with her over this—whatever "this" even was! I should be making better memories than this."*

Laura followed me out to the living room, but by then I'd changed my tune. For the first of a thousand times in my marriage to her, I wanted to be married more than I wanted to be right. My parents' legacy had saved me from my ridiculous self, and I was all too ready to make amends. It was an important about-face in the moment, and it would be important for years to come. Through financial stress and four miscarriages and the painful loss of Laura's mom—through so many trials over the years to come, we'd stay healthy and holy and whole. And it would be because of my dad's profound instruction that fascination is our *choice* to make. We are as fascinated with our spouse as we choose to be. I was learning to stay fascinated with mine.

Not who *are* you, but who are *you*—remembering that if I allow it, it's always new.

A few weeks ago my family was with a group of friends, and my dad started in on a story about a funny thing that happened to my mom and him during a recent flight they were on. They were heading to a benefit luncheon, my dad was explaining, and he'd just complimented my mom on what a lovely pantsuit she was wearing. As he continued on with the story, my mom sidled up to him and casually rested her hand in the crook of his arm.

My dad said, "Shirley had ordered tomato juice to drink, and evidently the flight attendant had placed it on the armrest between us, where there was a little rimmed area for your drink." I see my mom begin to chuckle now, even before my dad gets to the funny part. "I didn't see this tomato juice, you understand, and the next thing I knew, as I shifted in my seat to turn and ask Shirley a question, I inadvertently elbowed the plastic cup, causing it to go airborne, and then I watched in horror as at least half of that tomato juice landed right in Shirley's lap."

By now my parents both are laughing, along with their friends who had gathered around. My dad keeps going. "Which wouldn't have been so bad, except that that lovely pantsuit I mentioned? It happened to be *stark white*."

People are now falling apart in waves of hysteria, my parents numbered among them. I can't help but shake my head in admiration and laugh.

Once my dad regains his composure a little, he says, "Now, I'm not sure if you know this about me, but I have a bad habit of laughing at inappropriate times. And for some reason, seeing Shirls sitting there in that beautiful white suit, with big red splotches all the way down her legs . . . well, the scene just cracked me up."

He begins to snicker again even now. He knows where this story is going. "And right in the middle of my inappropriate laughter," he says, and then glances sheepishly at my mom, who finishes his sentence for him, "I poured the *rest* of that juice in *his* lap."

She rises on tiptoe in an attempt to give my dad a peck on the lips, but he'll have no part of it. "Oh, no, you don't," he teases. "Not after shenanigans like that!"

After the moment passes and their friends disperse to the dinner party, my dad pulls her into an adoring embrace. And as I stand there observing them from several feet away, I think, *This is what true love looks like. This is how true love behaves.*

They've been surprising each other since the beginning. For them, it's still always new.

finding your exceptional life

1. As you consider your relationship with your loved ones—your spouse or children, your parents or siblings, your in-laws who may feel like outlaws at times—do you more easily veer toward fascination or frustration? What realities factor into your tendency here?

2. In your experience, is it really possible to "choose to make it good," when it comes to intimate relationships? Why or why not?

3. How does God's promise that He is always making things new affect our ability to create newness in our relationships day by day?

10

remember the individual

It is only to the individual that a soul is given.

—ALBERT EINSTEIN

For nearly four years now, my dad and I have cohosted a daily radio program called *Family Talk*, aimed primarily at helping young families navigate modern culture in a biblical way. We work to present Judeo-Christian values in an accessible manner and spend nearly all our on-air time suggesting course corrections for families who need to be gently steered back to timeless truths and godly principles. (My own family certainly fits this bill.) My dad's four-plus decades of spiritual, clinical, and broadcasting experience converge with my kid-trapped-in-a-forty-something's body to form what I like to think is a highly enlightening, highly entertaining show.

Recently, he and I were recording a program about effective fathering—how to be a great dad, how to raise great kids, how to love well. Without fully intending to, I launched into a several-minutes-long spiel about how grateful I am for my dad, and also for my dad's dad. In the course of conversation, I brought up the fact that when I was growing up I used to hate being subjected to viewing my mom and dad's countless photo "slides"—you know, the ones that slip into the slots of plastic circular trays and that can bore a kid for hours. Sixty trays, my parents had. *Sixty.* It was awful.

A few years ago, a friend of my dad's decided to digitize all those slides, and sometime after that—nine or ten years ago, I think it was—I happened upon a copy of the disc containing the images. Interestingly, now that I had a little maturity on my side, I actually enjoyed seeing the shots. I would sit in front of my computer monitor, clicking through photograph after photograph, taking in those stills of my dad—then a young man—and his dad, enjoying each other, embarking on adventures, living life.

As the decades marched on, the shots of my dad and me over-took the scene, from when I was a baby and then a toddler and then a school-age boy and then a teen. But across the years, while the expressions changed and the styles changed and vibrant colors replaced black-and-white, one thing remained the same: there was delight all over the place. My dad's dad adored him, and Dad adored his dad; my dad treasured me, and I treasured him as well. As I took in all those old photos, I could see the intimacy there, the familiar, familial love between my grandpa and my dad, and between my dad and me. These relationships were and are far from perfect, of course. But there is mutual affection there that would be ridiculous to deny.

So, I'm relaying all of this for our audience that day, about how rich the relationships between the three generations of Dobson men were and continue to be, and about how I learn so much about how to enjoy my own son, Lincoln, simply by observing how the men before me practiced love. I finish my spiel and toss to my dad, who will then close out the segment. We conclude our remarks, and we're ready to move on. Or so I think. I look at my dad with a satisfied grin, a look that says, "Hey that was pretty cool." But the look I get in response doesn't jibe. Something is obviously on his mind.

"We need to do another piece on this subject," he says pensively. "There probably is somebody listening today who didn't have a great relationship with their father, or who isn't close to their child. We need to say something straight to them."

My dad goes on: "Not everybody has what we have, Ryan. I'd hate to pour salt in an already painful wound by relishing in our close relationship. I want to make sure the one who may feel unseen somehow today feels seen."

I was a little caught off guard. I mean, we'd just wrapped several minutes of *great radio*; didn't my dad get that? And yet at a deep level, I wasn't surprised. For as long as I've known him, my father has been hyper-concerned with the individual. Not the masses. Not the movements. But the single, solitary soul, the individual *person* doing his or her level best to live this thing called life.

"Remember the individual, Ryan," he'd always say. "It's the individual who counts."

Growing up, I had a rather adversarial relationship with the ministry my dad founded back in the 1970s, Focus on the Family. I was a son in need of his dad, and too often I felt "Focus" took priority over me. This wasn't Focus's fault, of course; my dad was responsible for his choices, and sometimes he chose work over me. Or that's how I saw it, anyway. Kids have a certain insatiable appetite for their parents' attention and admiration, and I was no exception. This remains true even for teenagers, I should tell you, even though they'd deny it up one side and down the other.

Anyway, I wanted my dad for myself; all of him, all the time. To my adolescent brain, I couldn't for the life of me sort out what could be worthy of so much of his energy and time, when there was a perfectly good kid at home (that would be me), to hang with and talk to and teach. It would take decades before I'd realize why my dad had invested in his "other" ministry the way he did.

I married my first wife one week before my twenty-fifth birthday and knew within forty-eight hours of my "I do" that something was terribly wrong. It would take nearly six years for my divorce to be final, and those were six tragic and painfully long years. The net result was that at age thirty I found myself without a spouse, without a job—I'd been fired from vocational ministry because my wife had filed for divorce—and without a plan for my life. My house and most of my money would soon be taken from me too as I mentioned before, but thankfully—maybe even by the grace of God—I didn't know that yet.

Around the same time as my world was coming unraveled, my dad's ministry was gearing up for what they called National Bike Ride for the Family, the largest cycling event of its kind in history. The idea was that cyclists from all over the nation would enlist financial pledges from friends and loved ones for the miles they'd ride across one of fifty self-contained state rides, and staffers from various ministries within Focus would sign up to ride several regions in a row. The final ride would take place in Colorado Springs, where Focus is based, and would usher in the ministry's twenty-fifth anniversary celebration. The entire trek took nineteen months and was beyond exhausting. I know because I did it.

Just before the event kicked off, my dad found himself in a real quandary. The guy who was supposed to spearhead things was a beloved colleague of my dad's who sadly was unable to do it for personal reasons. But the schedule had already been set, city-by-city events had already been planned, and scores of my dad's fans had already raised their monies and made their plans. The rides had to go on, even as there was nobody to lead the rides.

My dad and I were hanging out one afternoon, and he couldn't get his mind off the dilemma. "Ryan, I don't know what we're going to do," he said. "We've got to have someone who is young enough and athletic enough to ride a bicycle across this entire country, and who has enough discretionary time to commit to an endeavor such as this. *What are we going to do?*"

I stared at my dad incredulously and patiently waited for his eureka moment to arrive.

Sure enough, it did.

"Ryan!" he said, enlightenment at last showing up. "You! *You* could do it!"

I signed up for six events but wound up doing twenty-three. Those who were involved in the ride had been radically changed by the ministry my dad had begun. My father had enlisted the aid of a young, athletic guy named Brian to help run the program, and whenever Brian spoke of Focus's impact in his life, he couldn't help but get choked up. Here was a beast of an athlete—he could ride a thirty-four-day stint with only a single day of rest in the mix—and a tall, otherwise brawny man; and yet the mere mention of my dad's ministry would leave the guy wet-eyed and emotional.

My cynicism was at an all-time high back then—about Focus, about ministry, about life—and yet there was something so *genuine* about Brian's emotion. What did he know that I hadn't grasped?

At one of the events—in Wyoming, maybe?—a guy stood up to thank those of us there representing Focus for our ministry over the years. He was probably in his early eighties, and as soon as he made his way to the mic at the front of the room, I noticed a carotid artery scar that ran just below his left ear and down his neck. This was a man who looked like he'd had a rough go at life, but there was a tenderness to him as well. I was eager to hear what he'd say.

"Seven years ago, my wife died," he began. "And after that, I didn't want to go on." He explained how painful losing his wife had been. Hearing his story reminded me of Johnny Cash after losing his June.

Johnny Cash passed away just four months after his wife of thirty-five years, June Carter, passed away. Smart people in lab coats would say Johnny died from respiratory failure, that it was complications from his diabetes that took his life. But the watching world had to wonder: was it actually a broken heart that did him in?

I then noticed the mic start to shake vigorously in the man's hand, as he let out wave upon wave of tears.

I too couldn't help but cry. Here I was, a newly divorced man who was in debt up to my eyeballs and in the process of losing absolutely every material and relational asset I'd ever known. I had nowhere to go, nothing to do, and nobody to do it with. I was in a black hole, if ever there were one. Cynical about life. Cynical about ministry. Cynical about this stupid event. But then, then the man pulled it together a little and choked out the following words: "I wrote Focus on the Family and told them I was sad. And someone—they *wrote me back*."

He said that a few days after he'd mailed his letter, a woman from Focus called him and asked how he was doing. She prayed with him and said she was so sorry for his loss, and for his pain. And then she told him it was okay to be sad.

The following week, that same woman boxed up a bunch of my dad's books and a bundle of tapes of my dad's radio program and shipped them all to this man. She called him to make sure he received everything, and then she suggested a few chapters in those books that she thought would be most meaningful to him. She prayed for him again, and then steered him toward ideas for reestablishing some sense of community in his life.

The week after that, she called him again. And a week later, yet again. She stayed in touch with this man for months and months this way, until his sadness started to lift. He'd come to the event that evening for one reason, and one reason alone: to say thanks. "I'm alive today," he said, "and I'm not sad today, and it's this ministry I have to thank."

It was in that moment that my hard shell of cynicism cracked. Into a million tiny pieces, it cracked.

Remember the individual. It's the individual who counts.

Tim Ferriss, the entrepreneur and best-selling author of *The 4-Hour Work Week* (2007) has a concept he refers to as MED, or Minimal Effective Dose. The MED is the lowest volume, the lowest frequency, and/or the fewest changes needed in order to reach a desired result. For instance, when Ferriss's overweight dad was trying to drop some serious poundage and was told by Tim that the only thing he needed to do was consume thirty grams of protein within thirty minutes of waking each morning, he responded with a shocked, "That's *it*?"

It couldn't be as simple as *that*, could it?

"That's it," Tim confirmed for his father. "Don't make any other changes to your diet or lifestyle. Just drink a protein shake that will give you exactly thirty grams of protein—and no more—and do it inside the first half-hour you're awake."

According to Ferriss, this is the weight loss "MED." And according to Ferriss's dad, it works. After four weeks of doing exactly as his son had instructed, his average monthly fat loss skyrocketed from five pounds to nearly nineteen pounds, an increase for you non-mathematicians of *275 percent*. These results were simply astounding. And yet Ferriss was unfazed by the results: "Thousands of readers have lost ten to one hundred pounds and more using this approach," he said. "Simple works. Complex fails."[5]

Ferriss writes extensively on how this concept spans every facet of life. Want to be a good cook? Learn three techniques: braising, sautéing, and grilling. Want to be fluent in any language? Learn not an entire lexicon, but simply the thousand highest-frequency words. Want to be a marketing genius? Read Kevin Kelly's blog post "1,000 True Fans." On and on he goes, which got me thinking. If there is a MED for *everything*, then the way we live as lovers of God must have a proven MED too. When I consider ministry—that is, the vocational or avocational work of any follower of Christ to see God's kingdom reign here on earth—a clear MED comes to mind, courtesy of my dad: *Remember the individual.*

It's like I could hear my dad's voice whispering to me, as I listened that evening to the Johnny who had lost his June. "Remember the individual, Ryan. It's always individuals we're ministering to." In that moment, I knew he was right. Even Jesus said as much.

You and I both know the story of Jesus feeding the five thousand with two fish and five loaves of bread. But we rarely recall the context here—which is that Jesus first *saw the people there.* Mark 6:34 says, "When Jesus landed and saw a large crowd, he had compassion on them, because they were like sheep without a shepherd. So he began teaching them many things."

I think of my dad's rise to Christian fame of sorts and of how easy it would have been for him to never really, truly "see" the large crowds. Thankfully, he chose a different route. Despite what would have been easy to do, he chose the Jesus way. He saw—and *really saw*—the crowds. He saw to the point of having compassion on them.

Years ago, my dad stepped into an elevator that was occupied by a woman already standing inside. The woman did a double take as my dad pushed the button of the floor where he was headed and then said, "Excuse me, but are you Dr. James Dobson?"

After my dad said yes, she said, "My son is gay. Why do you hate my son?"

Talk about cutting to the chase.

My dad has this insanely admirable quality where even when he is being attacked, he refuses to attack back. He refuses to even defend. Had the woman said something like that to me, I probably would have countered with, "How dare you! What do you get off accusing me of such a horrible thing? Get a life, woman." Maybe I wouldn't have said it aloud, but *think* it? Ten times out of ten.

But not my dad. He doesn't entertain angry retorts. Well, maybe a few times he has, but not often. I can say this: It's not his default response.

I wasn't with him that day in the elevator, and while I don't know how he responded word for word, I can guarantee you this: he responded with love. Love for this woman, and love for her son. He can do this because he *gets* grace. He knows that this is a mom who is hurting, and that her son is hurting too.

Along the way, critics would say, "James Dobson is a gay-basher. He hates homosexuals." But it couldn't be further from the truth. In fact, the reason he wrote so extensively on the topic is because *the individual* is his greatest concern. And enough *individuals* had written to him over the years that he knew many *individuals* were living in great pain.

I used to ask my dad if it hurt, to be misunderstood like he has always been. "It does, but it's worth it if my work helps even one find healing," he'd say.

One.

It's always been about one.

Recently, my dad asked Becky, one of our colleagues who has been charged with managing "development" for our radio ministry, to go visit—in person—a few people who contribute significant sums of money to keep us on the air. My dad simply wanted to know their stories—who they are, and why they give.

Becky was my dad's personal assistant for eight years while he was at Focus and understands better than most this emphasis on individual hearts. But she is new to the world of development. What would she find, once she chose to dive in?

After consulting the giving records, she contacted a woman a few states away who had donated a large amount of money twice over a two-year span, and who on top of that had signaled her intention to contribute a small sum each month to keep our ministry afloat. Becky asked if she might pay the woman a visit when she was scheduled to be in her town, to which the woman agreed.

And so it was that Becky found herself in some random city one afternoon, knocking on an unknown woman's door. Nobody answered immediately, which is why Becky had time to notice all the bins of unopened mail sitting at the foot of the door. Eventually, the woman craned her head out the upstairs window and said, "Hang on! I'll throw down a key!"

Becky had no idea what that was about, but as instructed, she caught the key. She let herself into the woman's home and, along with her colleague, picked her way up the steps. Eventually, she sorted things out. The woman was clearly artistic and quickly explained that she had been housebound for twenty years. "I don't want to reach out to my brother," the woman said with a sheepish grin, "because he'll put me away in a home. And I don't want to go to a home. I want to stay here and paint."

The woman was a self-taught artist whose canvases adorned every wall.

After asking about the bins at the door, Becky learned that the woman had been getting old and weak. She couldn't retrieve her mail anymore; she couldn't even make it downstairs. But she'd inherited a large sum of money upon her parents' death, and she believed firmly in the message of our show. She'd given money to us even though she herself was in great need; *it's individuals we always minister to.*

Six hours after Becky and her colleague arrived at that woman's house, they had sorted her mail and lifted her spirits higher than they'd been in a long time. They learned that the woman had no Internet access and wouldn't mind a little CD player, so that she could listen to our program on disc. "Consider it done," Becky said with a wide smile. "My friend, consider it done."

When Becky returned and relayed that story, I thought, *Remember the individual, right? It's the individual we're ministering to.*

Just after my divorce, I decided to pierce my ears, despite my parents' disdain for the choice. But I was living on my own, and I owned my own home—what were they going to do? A few years later, I took the earrings out, and my mom shed actual tears. It's not that she'd loved me less with them in; it's just that the holes were so big I could stick my fingers in there, and she wasn't so sure about that.

Even deeper in my parents' rationale was this, though: they wondered if I wasn't unintentionally limiting my ministry scope— it was their tattoo theory reborn.

After I did the bike ride, requests for me to speak came flooding in, and as God put the pieces of my life back together, I sensed it was a door He wanted me to walk through. So I embarked on that season of flying all over the country and speaking at various ministry events. It was a role I dearly loved.

During that stint, a man wrote to my dad. He said, "Dr. Dobson, I saw your son speak last weekend. He has *earrings* in his ears. I'll never listen to you again."

I have to imagine that hurt my dad. Hadn't he raised me better than this?

Sure, he probably assumed the man was jumping to untrue conclusions, but he also knew I was doing that thing where you cut off your nose to spite your face.

It was around that same time that I decided to add to my collection of tattoos. And when I'm in short sleeves my art is visible. But here's what I have learned along the way: not only does the individual matter, he or she matters *a lot*. When my wife, Laura, and I decided to move from California to Colorado, and when I chose to head into ministry full-time with my dad, here is what I told him: "When I am ministering, I will wear long pants and long sleeves. I will let the message trump my method every time."

And I meant it.

Still today, whenever I'm speaking on behalf of Family Talk or any other ministry, I cover every last tattoo that I own (well, except my wedding band). Not because I am ashamed of them, but because they are not universally appreciated by the individuals who come hear me speak. It's something of a spiritual game of rock-paper-scissors to me; you've got to keep in mind what trumps what. Rock crushes scissors; scissors cut paper; paper covers rock. In the same way, *message trumps method every time.* The message God has given me to share means more to me than the aesthetic choices I've made along the way. It's all about the individual, remember? And the individual who will be kept back from my message because of my tattoos matters deeply to God and therefore must matter deeply to me.

Listen, I'm not going to get this right every time. I'll save batting a thousand for my dad. But this much I know is true: Because of Dad's influence, *I am aware.* And that represents crazy-wild progress for me.

Remember the individual, Ryan. It's the individual we're ministering to.

Yeah, I get that, Dad.

finding your exceptional life

1. When have you been treated as a number or a part of a movement, as opposed to an individual with distinct thoughts and feelings and a story that is all your own? What was the experience like?

2. Why is it easier to act from a place of judgment than a place of compassion in our typical, daily lives?

3. What might progress look like for you, in terms of remembering the individual at every turn?

11

you don't know what you don't know

*I don't think much of a man who is not wiser
today than he was yesterday.*

—ABRAHAM LINCOLN

We know a lot today. We know how to light houses with electricity, how to build aircraft that can transport us across oceans and around the world in increasingly short amounts of time, how to put astoundingly robust computing power no larger than the palm of your hand into the hands of 65 percent of the people on the globe, how to launch satellites into outer space, how to install fake organs in people's bodies that work almost as effectively as the real thing, and more. We know *tons* of stuff, and yet the list of what we don't know still laps all that we do know time and again.

My friend Annie specializes in multidimensional eye movement. Recently she completed her fifth certification in the field,
which is the highest you can go. During one of our conversations
she said, "You know, I find there are some interesting responses to
MDEM in pastors and teachers. If you ever want to do a session,
let me know."

Annie is the woman who introduced me to my wife, and
Annie and her husband are the ones who led Laura's and my premarital counseling. I like Annie. I trust Annie. And so I decided
to give it a go.

MDEM is based on a simple premise: When a human being
experiences certain types of pain or grief, neuropathways in the
brain become fragmented and no longer connect the way that they
should. Unless invited to reconnect, those pathways stay broken
for the rest of the person's life.

Annie is a professional reconnector.

She and I met one afternoon, and she asked me to have a seat
across from her, facing her, and just to relax. Which is more than
a little tough to do when someone is preparing to assess and then
fix your brain. Will it help? Will it hurt? Will I be worse off after
the session than I was when I arrived?

I noticed right away that Annie's primary "tool" for this
experience was a bundle of colored pencils, but without any lead.
Three-quarters of the rod was black and the final 25 percent was
a bright color—red or blue, yellow or green. She would custom
pick colors and then hold them at various points in my periphery.
She'd wave them ever so slightly and then watch what my eyes or
my nose or my lips did in response. You have to hold still while
she's doing all this, even as you let involuntary reactions have their

way, which for an ADHD guy like me is something south of easy. For the most part I felt very twitchy, like my entire body needed to sneeze.

Conversationally, things quickly got intense. Annie began asking questions about the babies Laura and I have lost to miscarriage these past several years—we had Lincoln seven years ago and then suffered a string of losses until Luci came along six years after Linc. She then asked questions about the loss of my first marriage, now more than a decade ago. Both subjects elicit great grief.

For a few moments I was highly self-conscious: What in the world are we doing here? How long is she going to keep waving these random sticks in my face? But then she moved the bundle of sticks near the bottom left side of my face and a tidal wave of tears flooded down from eyes to my cheeks to my neck. In a matter of seconds, the collar of my shirt was soaked. I hadn't cried that hard since we lost our first baby, almost exactly five years ago.

Annie wasn't done.

She slowly rotated the sticks as you would a volume knob on a stereo; when she rotated them one way my pain would intensify, while the other way would make the grief abate. She was turning on and off my emotional response like you flip on the light in a room. If I hadn't been there I wouldn't have believed it. What kind of voodoo party game was *this*?

"Stay with me, Ryan," she then said. "You can do this." Seconds later, she rotated the sticks again, she abruptly flicked her wrist, and she swooshed the sticks out of my line of sight. And *poof*, the pain was gone.

As in, *totally* gone. Pain I had wrestled with for the better part of twenty years: G-O-N-E, gone.

She looked at me and said, "How do you feel?" to which I said, "Good. And also like I could burst into tears yet another time if you did that whole routine again."

"Let's stay with this," she said. "Let me try one more thing."

She regathered a bundle of sticks and then she moved it to a different part of my face. She rotated it slowly, but it elicited no response. She then moved it down ten degrees, and like clockwork, I lost it again. Still without ever touching me, she then rotated it, flicked her wrist, and removed it from my line of sight. Again, the pain was gone. She began disassembling the sticks but then noticed a subtle twitch of my nose. "You reacted just then," she explained. "Hang on for just a sec."

She pulled the sticks back together, added a blue stick to the group, and then repositioned it near my face. *Bam*, another floodgate opened, despite my trying to keep my cool.

Annie and I continued with this process until I was twitch-free and grief-free and at peace. I got home that afternoon and my wife asked, "What in the world did she do to you?" The healing—it was written all over my face.

How does this work, you ask me? I do not know.

What I do know is that it does work.

And I know that there is far more I don't know in life than all I am certain of.

There's a line in Psalm 139 that is wildly profound but that has been so over-merchandised we've become a little biased about it. It says this: "I am fearfully and wonderfully made."

Think about that.

To find something truly "wonderful" or "fearful" is to be utterly *awestruck* by it, and the psalmist here is saying that *we*—the humanness that makes us *us*—are worthy of awe. The way we've been made ought to strike us with awe. In modern life, we tend to take ourselves for granted. We showed up on this planet with all these working parts—or mostly working, as the case may be—and we just assume that things will keep on ticking until our number is called and we head off to the by and by. But no, no, no. God's Word says, "Hang on a minute. *Look* at you. Don't you see it? Take a moment and just marvel, My friend. *You are wonderfully made.*"

God has designed us with intricacies and complexities we'll never comprehend. Oh, sure, we try: for example, last summer an initiative was completed in Europe and Canada in which researchers precisely mapped the brain; the Big Brain Project it is called. They wanted to better understand cell function and anatomy, but also how the brain's regions are distinct, and how these distinctions inform what happens in a diseased person. What is really going on in the brain of a man with Alzheimer's, for instance, or how does Parkinson's affect motor skill?

Researchers received a donated brain from a sixty-five-year-old woman and then shaved it into micrometer-thin slices. They mounted those slices on glass, stained them, and then scanned them into a computer, one at a time, nearly eight thousand slices in all. Who knows what data will flow from the studies they will do as part of this and a million future initiatives. This much I do know: we *still* won't know it all.

I wasn't sure I wanted to tell my dad about the colored-sticks experience I had with my friend Annie. My dad has a traditional background, and I wondered if he would think I was cuckoo for trying something that was by conventional standards a little "out there." But then I remembered something he said to me two decades ago, when I told him some of my buddies and I had decided not to go to college. My friends and I had just graduated from high school, and most of us didn't really see the need for further education. We felt we'd already paid our dues.

Dad looked at me and said, "Ryan, you don't know what you don't know."

Huh?

"Listen," he continued, "college is not just about coursework. It's about becoming a responsible adult. You have to learn to get along with a roommate you don't know, how to exist on a rigid schedule, how to live on a shoestring budget, how to get from point A to point B on your own . . ."

I looked at him with an expression that said, "You're not help-ing your please-go-to-college efforts here, with downer descrip-tions such as those."

Unfazed by my cynicism, he went on. "College is about tak-ing general-education classes that you see no purpose in but that might just spark something in you that says, 'I want to know more about that!' And then with that spark, you watch a raging fire erupt, as you find that thing you want to give your life to. But you don't get the fire without the spark, and you don't get the spark without inspiration. College is one place inspiration lives."

I understand now that my dad wasn't making a case for college attendance as much as for me to prize *learning* as much as he did.

He wanted me to see how satisfying it is to keep thirsting, keep seeking, keep trying, keep acquiring . . . to keep close at hand the indisputable fact that the only way to know is to know.

My dad has always been a dabbler. This is a man whose prevailing suppressed desire is to have enough discretionary time in his schedule that he can go to some collegiate campus and audit classes every day on subjects nobody has ever heard of. That about sums it up.

When I was a kid, he studied astronomy and then subsequently—with pen and paper and a clear understanding that existence is finite—mapped the entire universe "just for fun." I still remember looking at that handwritten map and vapor-locking. Who *does* stuff like this?

He'd turn an average Tuesday night family dinner into an intellectual spectacle by raising the question of whether the Big Bang Theory was in some important aspects exactly right. "If a black hole is prone to suck back into itself," he'd postulate, "then it's within the realm of possibility that the universe, if stretched to the point of its ultimate capacity, would give way and recoil onto itself too."

A few years later, he turned his voracious appetite for learning to another subject, World War II. Specifically, he wanted to understand the individual personalities at play that caused the war to ebb and flow and morph and shift and eventually be won. He was obsessed mostly with the leadership style of Winston Churchill: How could one man look at a cadre of fear-stricken all-but-defeated countrymen and rally them to overcome their darkest days? He read books and watched films and initiated conversations with very smart people, all in an effort to get his arms around the answer to that question. Something in him just *had* to know.

Today a giant oil painting of Churchill hangs just outside my dad's office, and to make mention of it in Dad's presence is to guarantee a twenty-minute impassioned spiel on the finer virtues of one of Britain's most famous wartime heroes.

And then there was art. My grandpa, James Dobson Sr., was a professional artist, and my dad definitely got hold of that gene. Though he never would claim to be "an artist," it was because of my dad that when my elementary school classmates and I were each sent home with a blob of smelly gray modeling clay and told to sculpt a squirrel, I was the sole student who returned with a squirrel. And a lifelike one, at that.

"People's faces are oval, not circular," Dad would tell me, when he saw me doodling smiley faces. He'd seize the pencil and gently restart my efforts, and then give me a quick lesson on proportion. "Here's where the eyes go, relative to the ears, you see? And look how the ears relate to the nose . . ."

For decades, every Sunday morning my dad would spend half the worship service sketching a perfect nautical five-point star. He was playing with depth and dimension—and he'd keep adjusting until it was just right.

My parents took my sister and me to countless musicals during our growing-up years—*Evita* and *Chess* and *Les Misérables* at least four times. Dad would carve out time in his increasingly busy schedule to expose me to the medical oddities museum and the medical war museum and the National Library, all in D.C. When revolutionary albums were released by The Beatles or The Beach Boys or The Mamas and the Papas, my dad would wax eloquent about the political implications of this "new music," and also about the uncustomary time signatures or the staggering lyrics or the drum beat that could just level you, it was so strong.

He would watch a boxing match on TV not passively but actively, explaining to me why it was so radical that Cassius Clay changed his name to Muhammad Ali and what it meant for religious freedom and racial justice that it was such a prominent athlete who'd done it.

My dad was interested in almost everything, and because of his magnetic personality and his childlike enthusiasm for making new discoveries, he could make you interested in everything too. I should know. I've had a bounce-off-the-walls personality since birth and required a lot of stimulation to be content. With Dad, I was always content.

To outside observers, it may appear that my father followed a linear path to his prowess: go to school, get your Ph.D., have a family, start a practice, and build a career. But with my dad, it wasn't like that at all. Yes, he did those things, but he did lots of other things too. And it has only been here recently that I've understood how those "other things" informed his "main thing."

The study of psychology has captivated my dad all his adult life. When he was getting his Ph.D. at the University of Southern California School of Medicine in the late 1970s, prevailing wisdom taught that children were born as blank slates, and that parents were 100 percent responsible for their kids' personality traits and behavioral profiles. In those days, it was all nurture, no nature. Or so people thought.

My dad came along and said, "No, no. Children do not happen on the scene as blank slates. They arrive with a certain percent of their personality *already intact*." Furthermore, at a time when beloved Dr. Spock wrote that parents should let their kids do whatever they wanted and then trust that those kids would grow up fine, my dad's book *Dare to Discipline* was released, which laid out the case for structure, spankings, and common sense.

Today, we accept these ideas as easy fact, but back then he rocked more than a few boats. Here was a professor of pediatrics— a guy who by all accounts was part of "the system"—going on record as standing against precisely what the system taught.

Yes, he was countercultural, but not whimsically so. My dad had studied these subjects; moreover, by then he'd already become a student of life. He had put actual thought into the big ideas of life—creation and reproduction and meaning and expression— and he had taken time to formulate his views.

He knew that you don't know what you don't know. He refused to be one who didn't know.

Growing up with a dad like that? I'd eventually see it for the gift that it is.

I've always been a natural questioner, one who doesn't typically accept someone's perspective just because they present that perspective persuasively. In this day of Wikipedia and the blogosphere, this inclination of mine typically serves me well; after all, it's *good* to have a little skepticism when wading through others' opinions and views. But here's a little secret I've picked up along the way, mostly by watching my dad: some people really know their stuff, and I'm wise to let their perspective sink in.

For example, when you pay a visit to your cardiologist and he talks about the problem with the ventricle in your heart, unless you also are a cardiologist, you don't get to say, "Well, I disagree. I think it probably works this way instead."

He is the scientist. And you and I are not. We do well to listen to what he says.

Likewise, my dad was always the student—always listening and learning—and I most often was not. It would take me a while, but I'd get there. I'd eventually let his perspective sink in.

When I was in my early twenties, I was over at a buddy's house and his dad was saying something about how "they" (whoever "they" were) were questioning whether six million Jewish people *really* were killed during the Holocaust. He said maybe that number was a little high. It's very embarrassing to recount this story, but later that day, I haphazardly mentioned the conversation to my dad in a know-it-all tone—like, "Yeah, maybe the 'experts' have been wrong all this time and we've just fallen for it, hook, line, and sinker."

This didn't go over well with my dad.

He didn't get mad. He just got serious. Very, very serious.

My father had devoted years to the study of World War II and to the tragic effects of Hitler's regime. He had read and researched and probed and assessed, and to think that his kid—at the time a skateboarder who rarely studied anything, *especially* history—was challenging anything about one of the greatest atrocities in the modern era was beyond him. "This is *not* something to split hairs over, Ryan," he said. "It dishonors every single one of those lives."

I didn't know what I didn't know. I was beginning to understand that now.

A few years into my dad's radio ministry, he came to a realization: Although the ministry he'd built was by all accounts thriving, it simply couldn't survive on the knowledge of just one man. "It will dry up if it has to rely on what's between my two ears," he said, and with that, he hatched a plan. He would elevate other thinkers, people who were studying as rigorously as he was. And that's exactly what he did.

Upon my dad's departure from Focus on the Family a few years ago, he was presented a plaque on which were engraved the names of forty-two organizations that had been founded or financially saved as a direct result of my father's influence. He had provided a platform for a thought-leader to convey his or her thoughts, and from there, things had taken off.

Fast-forward to a few weeks ago, when I was standing in our ministry's studio, preparing to record a segment that would air on our daily show. My dad was there, as were our two guests that day, one who is a former president of a seminary and a renowned author of more than twenty-five books, and one who has been a physician of pediatrics for nearly thirty years. Now, I can hold my own in conversation with these people, but in a moment of real clarity, I had eyes to survey the scene—and to see that scholastically and professionally, I was the undisputed lightweight in the room. But then this thought occurred to me: *What a wonderful place to be!*

To be the one who knows the least? It's here that humility has its way. It's here that you begin to learn.

finding your exceptional life

1. Would those closest to you describe you more as a know-it-all who has life figured out, or as someone with an insatiable appetite for learning everything you don't yet know? Would their assessment mesh with how you want to be perceived?

2. Do you agree or disagree with the idea that being in a position of vulnerability—in other words, being the scholastic and professional "lightweight" in a given situation—is a "wonderful place to be"? What personal experiences would you point to in supporting your answer?

3. What fears or concerns might keep you from placing yourself in a position of not having to know it all?

4. What excites you about coming into an even greater understanding of all that makes up this thing called life?

12

some things are worth fighting for

There are no pleasures in a fight, but some
of my fights have been a pleasure to win.

—MUHAMMAD ALI

I was raised by a fighter, which is probably why I love to fight. This didn't always serve me well, of course. As an adolescent, I'd take issue with something my mother would ask me to do, citing the very rational and thoughtful reason I shouldn't have to do it, and my father would look at me and say, "Your mom is right even when she is wrong, because she is your mom."

Telling that to a guy with a sky-high sense of justice always elicited an internal sense of rage. On the outside I'd comply, but inside I'd be shaking my head, thinking how unjust this treatment was.

Here is what my dad's comment back then was really saying to me: "Some things are worth fighting for, but this, young man, isn't one of them."

I now know that he was right. My dad *always* defended my mom, and she always defended him. This is the way it should be, isn't it? We all need someone to have our back.

In the winter of 1985, at the request of President Ronald Reagan, eleven United States citizens were commissioned to study over the course of one year all the dimensions of the problem of pornography.[6] They were to consider not only the legal aspects, but also the social, moral, political, and scientific concerns related to the industry. They were to evaluate its history, its market, its distribution, and its evolution over the past several years. They were supposed to assess the role of various people and institutions in the business of producing and disseminating pornographic material. They were supposed to examine the impact of consuming pornographic material on criminal or antisocial behavior. And then they were supposed to craft a list of recommendations based on their findings for changes the government should make.

My dad was one of those citizens. For him, it was a very long year.

When those twelve months had come and gone and the commission was preparing to present their report to the attorney general—a presentation that was to take place the very next day—a few members got cold feet. The report they'd put together was scathing—as any honest assessment of this deplorable industry would have to be—and those dissenting individuals suddenly wondered if the conclusions and recommendations would get them into trouble somehow. After all, the porn industry is a big, big industry—there's a lot of money in it, and therefore a lot of people stand to lose if the whole thing tumbles down. Furthermore, some of the people indicted by the commission's report were alleged leaders in organized crime—not exactly the types of folks you want to unnecessarily upset.

But didn't something have to be done? Their year-long investigation turned up absolutely wretched things: porn is addictive, porn is destructive, and porn carries with it all kinds of abuse. My dad would later say that after being made to view still shots and videos of such abhorrent behavior—sadomasochistic exchanges, as well as lewd episodes involving children, animals, and violence toward women—he would go back to his hotel room in whichever city the commission was meeting, he would sit on the edge of his hotel bed, and he would weep. I've asked him about those memories—about whether those images stick in a person's mind—and he doesn't say much in response. He shakes his head slowly, trying to find words.

Really, there are no words.

Countless millions of women, men, and children were suffering as a result of this terrible trade, and yet for the most part we as a society were simply looking the other way. My dad knew it. *Everyone* knew it. Yes, something had to be done.

Worried that the few dissenting voices would force the commission to wind up presenting a terribly watered-down version of the truth, my father phoned a few leaders at his ministry. He said, "Tomorrow, we pray."

I can't talk about what ensued without tears springing to my eyes. After that plea for prayer, the entire organization, which numbered more than four hundred people back then, ceased work activities and prayed. They asked God to intervene in the minds and hearts of the commissioned members, prompting them to deliver the *whole* truth back to the attorney general and, ultimately, to the president. And that's exactly what took place. One of the dissidents decided to stand with those on the commission who wanted their fully loaded report to find the light of day, and that was enough to sway the entire group to present the harsh realities the report contained.

I was a teenager when my dad served on that commission, and while I had the typical self-centered myopia characteristic of teens, I distinctly remember being aware that something big was going down in the Dobson household at the time. People were suing my dad for libel, such as the organizations that put out *Playboy* and *Penthouse*. Hugh Hefner was irate. Larry Flint published cartoon representations of my dad in his magazines that were inappropriate and very unkind.

It was then that my parents had a serious security system installed in our modest California home. Initially I thought it was beyond cool that infrared grids graced our front and back yards, but as weeks turned into months and credible threats kept rolling in, the novelty sort of wore off. My dad was stressed, my mom was worried, and I longed for the good old days, when every window of our house didn't boast jittery alarms waiting to scream.

The commission would present their findings, including their strong recommendations that a coordinated law-enforcement effort be enacted immediately to make sweeping legislative changes, train enforcement officers, and aggressively prosecute violators to the fullest extent of the law. My dad and his peers wanted change, and they wanted it now. They had labored long and hard, setting aside other pressing priorities, in order to devote themselves to this cause, despite the fact that "the cause" would subject them to untold headaches and heartaches. And they did all this because, in the words of my dad, "some things are worth fighting for."

Twelve years later, my father was commissioned to serve on another national commission, this time to study legalized gambling in all its forms—casinos, lotteries, dog and horse racing, video poker, sports betting, and Internet gambling among them—and then report back to the highest government officials what they believed the real threat was to gamblers and their families.

My dad was sobered by the mountain of evidence his colleagues and he quickly turned up. "Gambling is a destroyer that ruins lives and wrecks families," he said succinctly, summarizing their findings. He went on to explain that the commission had uncovered direct links between gambling and divorce, gambling and child abuse, gambling and domestic violence, gambling and bankruptcy, gambling and crime, and gambling and suicide. In fact, based on their research, the team found that compared with the other forty-nine states, the state of Nevada—considered the hub of gambling activity in this country—ranked *first* in the nation in suicide, in divorce, in high school dropouts, and in homicide against women. Nevada also came in third in bankruptcies, third in abortion, fourth in rape, fourth in out-of-wedlock births, fourth in alcohol-related deaths, fifth in crime, and sixth in the number of prisoners locked up. It ranked in the top one-third of the nation in child abuse and dead last in voter participation. One-tenth of all southern Nevadans were alcoholics, and in the

Las Vegas Yellow Pages, more than one hundred and thirty pages were devoted to advertising prostitution by its various names.[7]

None of this necessarily surprised my dad; he'd seen the ill effects of gambling on people's lives for decades. What did surprise him was that kids now were involved. The commission's findings proved that two-thirds of teens in 1997 had gambled that year, and that the subtle marketing ploy shifting the name from "gambling" to "gaming" was luring younger and younger bait into its grip.

He and his peers could find nothing redeeming about the practice of habitual gambling. Far from it; the opposite was true. In a letter he wrote to his radio-ministry supporters the same year the commission presented its findings, he noted the eventual effects of gambling, citing "creeping poverty, family disintegration, business failure, fraud, and other serious social ills."[8]

Given his life mission of serving the institution of the family, he was more resolved than ever to see the commission's recommendations take effect. He desperately wanted people to know that it was God who meets our needs, not a slot machine, and that the Bible commends hard work, not playing the odds. There was a better way to live than what gambling addicts were choosing. He wanted to show them that better way.

And yet for a contribution such as that, there would be a steep, steep price to pay.

While the verdict still is out regarding just how much of the porn industry is backed by organized crime, there really is no debate about such backing in the gambling world. The "credible threats" my family had received back in 1985 looked like child's play compared with the level of danger my father put himself in during his time on the gambling board. You know that when you're on the FBI's speed dial things are heating up a bit. Federal agents and local police officers alike were contacting us frequently, providing updates on the most recently discovered threats. We were told to "watch ourselves" and to "use extreme caution" and to stay home as much as we could.

People living in darkness don't like the light much. A lot of people didn't care for my dad.

And yet still, he showed up at every commission meeting, unyieldingly bent on uncovering truth.

Some things are worth fighting for. For my dad, this was worth the fight.

In 2003, my father made national headlines yet again, when he publicly defended Terri Schiavo's right to life on his radio program. You probably recall that there was a long, drawn-out, and very visible legal battle over whether to provide life support for Terri, who had suffered a cardiac arrest in her Florida home in 1990 that led to massive brain damage. She spent more than two months in a coma and then went through several years of speech and physical therapy while still being fed through a tube.

The controversy stemmed from Terri's husband wanting to remove the feeding tube and Terri's parents demanding it be kept in. The back-and-forth was ridiculous, as one court decision would cause the tube to be removed, followed by an appeal a few days later, which would force the reinsertion of the tube. The process was unconscionable, inhumane, and clear proof that our legal system needed an overhaul.

For this and many more reasons, my dad was simultaneously angry and sad. Which is why he was so relieved when it appeared the Florida court system had finally come to its senses for once. In October 2003, Governor Jeb Bush passed "Terri's Law," giving him the authority to save Terri from the court-invoked dehydration she had been dealing with for an entire week. "I just don't know why it took so long for the Florida Legislature to act," my dad said on his broadcast. "I mean, this is absolutely unbelievable situation . . . where a woman who's not in a coma—she's not on a respirator, she can relate to her mother and those around her, she can even say some words—[was] being starved to death, deprived of water [and food].

"It's her husband's statement that she didn't want to be on life support," he continued, "but she's not on life support. You know, if you're going to start killing people like Terri, you're going to have to kill an awful lot of people who are mentally retarded and/or on a feeding tube."

My dad was outraged, and justifiably so. "This situation will grab your heart," he said to his audience that day. "If you've ever gone a full day without drinking water, you can imagine what she's experienced after six days without food or water. It's Nazi-esque. It's what [Nazi Germany] did in 1939, '40, '41 and on through the war [to the disabled, to Jews, and to others]. It's where they started."[9]

Of course there were those who agreed with my dad that day and those who vehemently took the other side. It didn't surprise me to watch him stand his ground; I've been watching him do so all my life. Plato once said, "When you fight with faith, you're twice armed." My dad was teaching me to live twice armed.

There is an almost indescribable, positive impact on a son when he sees his father engage in the right fights. Not all fights are "right" fights; I learned this the hard way, of course. I can recall half a dozen or so real, actual, fist-to-face fights I was involved in as a teenager that I had no business engaging in. I even knew at the time it was stupid, but it would take some maturity before I would stop.

I'd also seen my dad refrain from engaging, when it wasn't the right fight. When I was in junior high I was suspended for talking too much, a penalty I found totally unjust. I raced home to tattle to my dad, just *sure* he'd take up my cause. But that's not how things would go down. He told me that while he agreed the punishment didn't fit the crime in my case, he planned to let the suspension slide. He then added, "And I advise you to do the same."

Which meant, "Suck it up and act like a man."

Like the vast majority of decisions my father made on my behalf along the way, the passage of time would help me see that he got it right. At the time, my dad's radio program was heard by one in three Americans and was one of the most powerful Christian voices nationwide. What he knew that I couldn't yet grasp was that if "the" Dr. James Dobson trotted down to that little Christian school I attended at that time, and puffed out his chest at my teacher, who was making a pittance in salary and was doing the absolute best she could to maintain some semblance of control in her classroom, she would never regain the authority that one conversation would cause her to lose.

Clearly, this wasn't the right fight.

Decades later, when he would depart his post at the ministry he had founded, he would choose not to jump in the fray of speculation about what "really" happened to cause him to leave. I so badly wanted him to retaliate, to defend his honor and explain his side, but time and again he said calmly, "Ryan, it's not the right thing to do."

I'd look at him slack-jawed. What kind of relationship does a man have with his God that he can take a public beating and not fight back? "It would hurt the kingdom and cause division," he would say. "You've got to know when it's not the right fight."

Well, as I still am trying to learn, the "right" fights, as informed by my father's influence, are ones not that protect our preferences, but rather our principles, our family, and our faith. To that latter issue, the right fights by definition protect people who simply can't fight for themselves. I think about this a lot these days, about how I surely hope there would be people standing up to fight for me if I were incapable of fighting for myself.

A few months before my twentieth birthday, I attended the Rally for Life pro-life event with my dad, at the time the largest political gathering that ever had taken place in Washington D.C.'s two-hundred-year history. National Park Service estimates counted seven hundred thousand attendees, but looking out over the crowd that day, I'd say there were well over a million people there.

The event took place just days after my dad turned fifty-four years old, and as he took the podium to deliver his remarks, the crowd began an impromptu rendition of "Happy Birthday to You." Once they'd finished their serenade, my dad, all smiles, said, "In my fifty-four years, this is the most beautiful sight I've ever seen."

He meant those words deeply. The right to life is a cause that courses through his veins.

In his commanding style, my dad acknowledged that pro-choice advocates indeed held all the power in the country at the time—the universities, the Congress, the public-school system, the medical and legal professions, all the centers of power in psychology, sociology, and business, but that we, those who were determined to fight for life, had the *people*. And though they weren't all gathered that day, we numbered in the millions—millions upon millions of people who were willing to speak for those who did not yet have a voice.

My father drew an analogy that day. "The start of the Civil War began with a bad Supreme Court decision," he said, "and before the fight was settled and the smoke had cleared and black Americans at last were declared free, at least six hundred thousand men were forced to lay down their very lives.

"This too is a civil war. And it will not be won by our staying in the safety of our living rooms, making an occasional phone call to a congressman. It will require the same level of dedication and commitment as our forefathers showed when they went into battle. This one isn't fought with grenades and cannons and guns, but on the battlefield of ideals—held at the ballot box and in our public schools and in vacant Supreme Court seats."

As that massive crowd applauded my dad's comments, he then said this: "I make a commitment to you here today, a commitment I ask you to consider as well. For the rest of my life, as long as God lets me live, I will never cast *one* vote for *any* man or woman who would kill *one innocent baby*."

My own chest nearly burst with pride for my fighter of a father that day. He exited the stage, and then our little group headed to an RV nearby, so that we could mop off the sweat from the hot, humid day and remove the bullet-proof vests we'd been asked by Secret Service to wear. Prior to the event, I remember asking one of the agents if we really needed to take such extreme measures to ensure our safety, to which he said, "There's at least half a million people out there, Ryan. Which means we can't check everyone. No matter how good we are, you'll still be in big-time danger. I'm going to insist that you wear the vest."

It was wise counsel that is instructive to me today. Fighting the good fight isn't for the faint of heart, but it doesn't mean it's not worth the fight. "Who may dwell in your sanctuary?" the psalmist asked God in Psalm 15. "Who may live on your holy hill?" (v. 1).

And then, answering his own questions, he lays it on the line. "He whose walk is blameless," he writes, "and who does what is righteous, who speaks the truth from his heart and has no slander on his tongue, who does his neighbor no wrong and casts no slur on his fellowman, who despises a vile man but honors those who fear the LORD, who keeps his oath even when it hurts, who lends his money without usury and does not accept a bribe against the innocent. He who does these things will never be shaken" (vv. 2–5).

I don't think my dad has been shaken a single day of his life.

finding your exceptional life

1. What makes a cause worth fighting for, in your view?

2. Have you ever invested yourself in a "wrong" fight? What were the results? What right fights are you invested in today?

3. Which part of Psalm 15 is most compelling to you, and why?

13

your yes has got to be yes

*It takes twenty years to build a reputation
and five minutes to ruin it. If you think
about that, you'll do things differently.*

—WARREN BUFFETT

When I was in the process of launching my first broadcast ministry about a decade ago, my dad approached me about one of my business associates, saying he "had some concerns." I had told my dad that the man had failed to make good on a few things he said he would do; and while the commitments weren't high-stakes in nature, to my father, it was a serious red flag. He said, "Ryan, the people you entrust yourself to will either add to or take away from your reputation. Their contribution is never benign."

It would be insights such as this one that would tell me along the way that my dad was not a good man, but a *great* man. Only great men think such great thoughts.

If my associate's "yes" wasn't truly yes when the stakes were low, as my dad's supposition went, did I really want him around when the stakes were high? George Washington once said that it is better to be alone than in bad company, a sentiment my dad surely espoused. I disconnected myself totally from the associate in question and have never regretted the decision once.

The "let your yes be yes" idea comes from the Sermon on the Mount, the lengthiest, most penetrating sermon Jesus delivered during His earthly ministry, and is recorded in Matthew 5, 6, and 7. Tucked between exhortations regarding heavy-hitting subjects such as divorce and adultery and murder and why you should love people who hate you back, Jesus says this regarding the importance of keeping your word:

> Again, you have heard that it was said to the people long ago, "Do not break your oath, but keep the oaths you have made to the Lord." But I tell you, Do not swear an oath at all: either by heaven, for it is God's throne; or by the earth, for it is his footstool; or by Jerusalem, for it is the city of the Great King. And do not swear by your head, for you cannot make even one hair white or black. Simply let your "Yes" be "Yes," and your "No," "No"; anything beyond this comes from the evil one. (5:33–37)

Much has been written through the centuries about what Jesus meant here, but for me the key takeaway is that, simply, we should be people of our word.

In first-century Jerusalem, the audience to whom Jesus was speaking, there was an elaborate system of oaths. For instance, swearing "by heaven, the earth or the sun was not considered to be an oath," but swearing toward Jerusalem, "the temple, the altar, sacrifices, and the life of one's head" was.[10] Jesus was saying, "Hey, here's an idea. *Don't swear at all.* Let your yes be yes and your no be no. Just be people of your word."

We're guilty of the same thing those earlier followers did: little girls "pinky swear" on the playground that they'll be best friends forever; we burden an agreement with layers of assurances, saying "you have my word on that"; we don't think twice about seeing a witness place his hand on the Holy Bible and swear to tell the whole truth and nothing but the truth, so help him God. In fact, if any significant portion of us actually *practiced* this yes-be-yes thing, the entire legal profession would vanish in the night.

Can you imagine what might unfold in our world if those who inhabit it lived as people of their word?

My wife used to be part of a ministry that preached a motto to its workers: *results show intentions.* She says it stemmed from employees of the ministry perpetually being late for work. The leader of the organization pulled together the team and said, "Listen, if I offered to pay you a million bucks to be on time every day for a year, I think you'd find a way to be on time. Let's quit talking about our good intentions and let our *results* be the measure of our success."

Those employees had signed on to work for the ministry, fully aware that they were expected every morning at eight. Their boss simply was suggesting they make good on that initial "yes."

When I was a kid—as young as nine or ten—my friends used to give me a hard time about my inability to tell a lie. A bunch of my buddies were playing a joke on a mutual friend one time and told him the principal of our school wanted to see him and that he was probably in really big trouble. They really got him worked up, and just as he was about to break a literal sweat, he turned to me and asked, "Ryan, is this for real?"

It was all over then. To my buddies' deep dismay, I'd squeal like a stuck pig. "Aw, man!" they'd groan. "You ruin it *every* time!"

They were absolutely right. I *would* ruin it every time, and it's all my father's fault. If there was one thing you didn't do in the Dobson home, it was willfully tell a lie. If you made a promise, you kept it. If you agreed to do it, you did it. If you said yes, you'd better have meant yes. Following this overriding principle made me uncool as a kid and threatens my well-being still today.

Laura and I were on vacation last year, and partway through our trip she looked at me and asked, "Do you like my hair like this?"

I studied her hair for a second and then dispassionately answered, "Nope."

She was incredulous. We've been married all these years, and she finds my candor shocking still.

The next day, she said, "You know, when I asked about my hair, I don't think I wanted an honest answer," to which I smiled and said, "Then you shouldn't have asked the question."

I pulled my wife into a hug and tried to explain that it was nothing personal; it's just that she's a beautiful woman with fantastic hair, and that particular hairstyle didn't do it justice. "It's not a good look on you, that's all," I clarified, but the damage had already been done. She blew me off with a playful shrug and hasn't asked me about her hair again since.

What I lack in diplomacy, I make up for in delivery: ask me an honest question, and you'll get an honest answer, 100 percent of the time. There are worse things to be known for, I figure, than a no-nonsense, straight-shooting man. Eight years ago, I gave my "yes" to my wife, Laura, and even as the divorce rate hovers just above 50 percent, that yes is one I fully intend to keep. My yes means she can count on me, that I'll remain faithful and supportive and kind.

I've also given yeses to my children, to Lincoln Cash and Luci Rose. I've said yes to protecting them and providing for them and teaching them about life and about God, and you'd better believe I will honor those yeses, all the days of my life.

I've given yeses to my mom and my dad and my sister along the way, to defend their honor and add to their reputation instead of putting them in personal or professional jeopardy by behaving like a fool. Clearly, I haven't hit the mark every time, but my heart is in the right place. I know, I know, *results show intentions.* Let's say I'm a work in progress here—an arrow pointed at the right target, at least.

Several years ago, my sister and I received a contract from a publisher, for a book on "growing up Dobson." Per the attached cover letter, they wanted to understand the sweetness of our "classic American family" and also how we as Dr. Dobson's children overcame the challenges fame tends to bring.

Danae and I considered the offer and even scheduled a call with the publisher to discuss some of the fine print. Which is when she and I both discovered that what was really being sought was dirt. The publisher was in the hunt for a little scandal, and they hoped we could deliver for them. Before shredding the contract, I explained that even if there were salaciousness to report—and there isn't—the last thing my sister and I ever would do is throw our beloved family under the bus.

Of course our family's relationships are not perfect, but *we have each other's backs.* We've given each other our heartfelt yeses— yes, I will love you; yes, I will speak truth; yes, I will honor God with my life—and we intend to be people of our word.

Our yeses *matter.* They matter to our loved ones, and they matter deeply to God. And I suppose if I had to net it out, this is why the issue always carried great weight with my dad. Remember that Bible verse about God trusting people with big things who had been faithful to steward the small stuff well? Jesus is teaching His disciples the value of shrewd living by way of a parable and says in summary, "Whoever can be trusted with very little can also be trusted with much, and whoever is dishonest with very little will also be dishonest with much. So if you have not been trustworthy in handling worldly wealth, who will trust you with true riches? And if you have not been trustworthy with someone else's property, who will give you property of your own?" (Luke 16:10–12).

Typically, this passage is taught with a singular emphasis on money, but for my dad, the lesson reached further than that. Because he made a living filling radio airwaves, he considered his greatest currency not bills and coins, but rather *words.* To him, to be "trusted with true riches," as the passage in Luke 16 suggests, was to be given broader reach—more listeners, more hearts, more souls. To be invited into people's lives for the sole purpose of explaining the nature of God and His divine plan for the family unit, which God had patterned after Himself, was for my father an unspeakable gift, a sacred entrustment to be carefully held.

There's a lesson here for you and me both. I relate easily to my dad's perspective because I too make a living on the air. But for *all* of us who claim to love Jesus, I think there's a clear takeaway. As we make good on our promises in daily life, we practice being truth-tellers in weightier ways. When I agree to stop by the grocery store for my wife on my way home from work and then actually remember to stop by the store, I put another tick mark on the side of the ledger that says I'm a man of my word.

When I tell Lincoln, "Yes, son, I'll be at your baseball game tomorrow," and then actually show up for the game, another case is made for my being a reliable man of my word.

When I look my dad in the eye and say, "Sure, Dad, I'd love to speak at that event," and then I show up ready to deliver a passionate talk, the "man of his word" side of that ledger starts to tip over because there are so many tick marks adding up.

With every seemingly minute decision, my reputation is getting built. Either I'm known as a man whose yes is truly yes, or I'm not. There's not much in between.

One of the most famous of all Aesop's Fables is of the boy who cried wolf. As the story goes, a shepherd boy tasked with watching the village sheep grew bored there on the hillside one day and decided to have some fun. He took a big breath and shouted at the top of his lungs, "Wolf! Wolf!" just to see what people would do.

As expected, the villagers came running to help the boy rescue the sheep from the wolf. But of course there was no wolf, and the boy laughed that they'd fallen for his prank.

"Don't cry wolf when there's no wolf!" said the villagers to the boy, and then they went grumbling back down the hill.

Later, the boy did it again. "Wolf! Wolf!" he shouted, causing the villagers to come running once more. They realized that there was no wolf this time either and went grumbling back down the hill.

Yet a third time, the boy cried out. "Wolf! Wolf!" he said. "A wolf is chasing the sheep!" But this time, no one came running. They knew better than to believe the boy. The trouble was, this time there really *was* a wolf, who really *was* threatening the village sheep. The moral of the story? According to translator William Caxton, who standardized the tale for an English-speaking audience, "Men bileve not lyghtly hym whiche is knowen for a lyer."

Our yes has got to be yes.

finding your exceptional life

1. What situations, circumstances, relationships, or dynamics make it most difficult for you to "shoot straight" in conversation? What fears tend to hold you back?

2. When have you allowed your "yes" to be yes, even when it would have been far more convenient to lie?

3. How would those who know you best characterize your faithfulness in speaking truth, regardless of the cost?

14

nothing wrong with
a little friendly competition

*I am too positive to be doubtful. Too optimistic
to be fearful. And too determined to be defeated.*

—Unknown

I t's my dad's fault that I am hyper-competitive. I grew up under the tutelage of a wicked smart, wildly athletic, incredibly accomplished, deeply inspired, formally trained artist/theologian/ savant—what else could I do but try to get good at stuff too? *Especially* stuff he himself hadn't mastered. When I learned that my dad couldn't sing, I began performing in theater productions. When I learned he was afraid of heights, I became an overnight

rock-climbing pro. But then he took me to see professional musicals, and he agreed to rappel with me not once but multiple times
off of an eleven-hundred-foot-high sheer-faced rock wall called
The Prow in Yosemite Valley.

Hmph.

When I entered my freshman year of college, a thought
occurred to me. I had been working too hard to beat my dad at
his own game—or *games*, actually—instead of finding something
he couldn't do and excelling at it before he knew I'd even acquired
the skill. I'd get good, and I'd get good *fast*, which according
to Malcolm Gladwell is an effective way to win. "[Great] power
can come [from] substituting speed and surprise for strength,"[11]
he writes, referring to the means by which history's most classic
underdog, the shepherd boy David, defeated the intimidating
giant, Goliath.

Enter Ping-Pong.

Despite the fact that my dad was the captain of his college
tennis team and frequently throughout my growing-up years took
quiet pleasure in absolutely burying any of my sister's boyfriends
who had the audacity to challenge him to a match—"How good
can he be?" they'd posture. "He's an old man, and I still have
legs."—I decided to take up a sport involving a racket (okay, a
paddle), a round ball, and a net.

Early in my college tenure I happened to meet the campus
Ping-Pong campus champion, who decided to take me under his
wing. He also was named Ryan, and after a few months of his
insightful instruction, although he still was the best in school
by a mile, I had skyrocketed to number two. I returned for my
sophomore year and thought things were going smoothly, until

Ryan informed me matter-of-factly that he had changed his grip over the break.

I'd learned to play table tennis using the Chinese "penhold" grip, holding the paddle as you would a spoon, and got really, really good at the style. But now Ryan had switched to the American and European "shakehand" grip, stating, "It's a better way to control the ball, and you'll be a better player once you adapt."

Furthermore, as is the custom of so many annoying foreign-language teachers who refuse to let you speak anything but that foreign language in their classroom, Ryan informed me that he would no longer play with me until I adopted the shakehand grip.

In the end, I changed my grip. And my junior year, after Ryan graduated, I went 32–0 in the tournament hosted by my school. I *slayed* it. Ryan was absolutely right: the new grip was serving me well. And, Ryan Myers, if you're reading this I'd like a shot at the crown sometime.

Well, evidently I was paying so much attention to my burgeoning Ping-Pong career that I allowed my grades to slide a bit. Actually, they slid a lot. They slid so much, as you'll recall, that I got myself kicked out of school. Which was a bittersweet experience, because, while it was humiliating to have to tuck tail and head back home to live with my parents, who now resided in Colorado Springs, I arrived back home a Ping-Pong *master* who finally found something I could do better than Dad. There was no question in my mind I could beat him; the only question was how severe those beatings should be.

I puffed out my chest and exhaled great pride and even used Bible verses to bolster my wins. All the metaphors about "running the race" and "wrestling well" and "fighting for the prize"? Clearly even God Himself was on my (victorious) side.

It would be years and years before I'd come to the sobering realization that while I may have won the Ping-Pong battles, I'd lost the Christ-following war.

Historically there has been a key difference between my dad's style of competition and mine, not dissimilar to the difference between a steamroller and a feather duster. It's not that my dad isn't fiercely competitive; he is. He's just adept at keeping the "friendly" in "friendly competition," whereas I, I just am not.

I was born bad-competitive, angry-competitive, the kind of competitor nobody wanted to take on—not because of an admirable win-loss record, mind you, but because I was *vicious*, come victory or defeat. I had a fight-to-the-death mentality that would only get tempered by my well-tempered dad. One thing is certain: When you watch a good sport be a good sport time after time after time, you tend to want to be a good sport too.

I look back over the years my dad and I have competed, and I see a common and convicting thread. He's always ensured I've been set up for success, even if I didn't happen to win that day. Case in point: one elk hunt in particular.

For decades, my father and I have hunted together, engaging in a sport that is near and dear to both our hearts. We've been to exotic locales and out-of-the-way hunters' paradises and have some incredible tales to tell. But here's the thing with hunting: you wait a long, long time to see game appear, and then *still* you may not get your kill. We've had our share of busts on various trips, where we sat for days and caught not one thing.

It's for this reason I was so moved, so *astounded*, when my dad handed over the first good shot. We were elk hunting in Wyoming at a place that wasn't cheap to hunt, and on day one of this once-in-a-lifetime experience, I overheard my dad whispering to our guide. "Make sure Ryan gets the first bull," he was telling him. "Line him up before even *thinking* about me."

I couldn't believe my ears.

My dad is over-the-top competitive. He had forked over a wad of cash to foot this bill. Depending on conditions, there might only be one good shot all day. And my dad was reserving that kill for me.

I was over thirty years old when this happened—I owned my own home, even—and yet my dad still was looking out for me. We would leave that lease a few days later, me with a monstrous bull elk trophy, and my dad with nothing more than an old, ugly, pathetic one-horned catch. We joke about that elk still today.

Here's the part I took very seriously: my father enjoyed my victory as much as if he'd harvested that trophy himself. I learned a lot about healthy competition that day.

Five years later, I'd get a chance to live what I'd learned. My dad and I departed Denver, Colorado, and flew to Minneapolis-St. Paul and then to Saskatoon, Saskatchewan, and then to La Ronge, where we boarded a float plane and headed to a place four hundred miles south of the Arctic Circle called Black Bear Island Lodge.

At Black Bear Island Lodge, where their motto is, "All you have to do is get to La Ronge!", you are treated to some of the best fishing and bear hunting Canada has to offer. Days were spent catching biblical amounts of walleye, great northern pike, and bass, all of which the guides would fry up shore-side for lunch, and evenings were spent sitting in hunting stands, waiting on the coveted black bear. It was a rhythm I couldn't have loved more.

I'd asked to hunt alone during the evenings because I tend to talk a lot, and bears don't come around when they hear chatter. My guide would stick me on a small boat, point me an hour and a half away from camp, and say, "I'll trail you in a bit. When dusk comes, if you've got something, take your orange hat, put it on a stick, and I'll come pick you up."

My self-controlled father, fully able to control his tongue, was allowed to hunt with a guide.

One evening, my dad and his guide were up in the stand, which sits nearly twenty feet in the air, when they noticed the stand beginning to sway a little, as though they were catching a steady breeze. The guide looked back at the brackets that bolted the stand to the trees and said, "Looks like we've got trouble. We need to get down . . . and *fast.*"

My dad quickly unloaded his gun, scrambled down the ladder, and exhaled relief once his feet touched the ground. The guide followed shortly after, repositioned the stand properly, and then headed back up to bolt everything in.

Once it was apparent what the problem was, as well as what the guide would need to do to fix it, a substantial amount of banging and clanging ensued as the guide set about his work. *Well,* my dad thought, *this day is a bust. No way is a bear going to come around here now.*

He stood idle at the base of the stand and then eventually reloaded his gun, figuring he'd better be safe than sorry, out here on prime black-bear-hunting grounds. No sooner had he dropped in a single bullet than a black bear emerged from the trees.

Here, my dad had a choice to make. Should he shoot? Run? Scream?

Instead, he kept his feet planted and had a little conversation with himself. "Huh. Would you look at that? Beauty of a black bear. But is this one big enough to shoot? I'd hate to shoot this bear reflexively and then realize later on that it's actually tiny . . . I'd catch heat from all my friends (and son)."

Bears have terrible eye sight but a fantastic sense of smell, and this bear had picked up a scent on my dad. Still standing about forty feet away from my father, the bear pointed his nose skyward and sniff-sniff-sniffed to the left. And then he sniff-sniff-sniffed to the right. He took one step forward and then did it again, sniffing the air around him, left and right.

The guide was still up in the stand, completely oblivious to what was unfolding two stories below. He had exactly no idea that either Dr. James Dobson or a black bear of unconfirmed size was about to meet an untimely death. He was still banging, still clanging, while the bear stood there utterly unfazed.

Just then, the bear shuffled forward another two steps—now fifteen feet away from my dad. Two quick gallops, basically, and my dad would be absolute toast.

Thankfully, better judgment prevailed, and my dad then eased his legs into firing position. *If the bear comes any closer,* he reasoned, *I'll have no choice but to shoot.*

The bear sniffed the air once more, took a large step toward my dad, and then never walked again.

When the sound of the shot reverberated through the trees, the guide almost fell out of the stand. "What in the world are you doing?" he hollered at my dad, followed by, "Oooh," upon seeing the bear. That bear was a full three hundred and fifty pounds, by the way—one of the biggest bears bagged by the resort that year.

That bear remains proudly mounted on a wall in my parents' home.

When my dad came back to the lodge the day of the kill, he learned that I too had made a good shot, and then we swapped stats on the kills we'd made. Letting the details sink in, he then looked at me and said, "Wait, is your bear *bigger* than mine?"

I grinned a little too eagerly and mouthed, "Yep!" with chutzpah to spare, to which my dad chuckled, folded his arms across his chest, and under his breath mumbled, "Well, you don't have to say it that quickly."

Fortunately, I made a decent recovery, remembering all my dad has taught me over the years. "Dad," I said, "I may have gotten the bigger bear today, but you got the bigger story."

I'm learning that the other guy doesn't have to lose for me to win, that competition can be friendly in the end. It's a good way to approach a bear hunt. And it's a good way to think about life.

finding your exceptional life

1. What conditions tend to spark your competitive side? Would others characterize you as friendly or unfriendly when you're in such a mode?

2. When have you been on the receiving end of competition that was friendly? What was the experience like?

3. What does it say about a person when he or she is able to create win-win situations instead of win-lose?

15

words have power

A word to the wise ain't necessary.
It's the stupid ones that need the advice.

—BILL COSBY

The day I received the most memorable spanking of my life was the day I learned the power of the spoken word. When my sister, Danae, and I were adolescents, we tossed verbal grenades each other's way pretty consistently; and during one of those snarky battles, I said words that cut right to her heart. They were hateful words. Harmful words. Words I knew I'd pay dearly for. I knew this because just as the barbed comment flew out of my mouth, my dad happened to be entering the room. Ah, timing is everything. That time, my timing stunk.

My dad once wrote a pretty popular book titled *Dare to Discipline*. My hindside can attest to the fact that he was feeling especially daring that day.

Of course, the spanking was deserved; my dad had taught me to behave better than that. What's more, he'd taught me to *be* better than that. This is what would take me some years to fully comprehend, that my words are a reflection of *who I am*. And by voicing the things that float through my mind, I can either build people up or tear them down. Words always are creative; with them we create goodness, or else we create what's bad. My dad has always maintained that it's far better to create the good.

Several years ago, my dad and I were on another elk hunt—this one in western Colorado—with a close friend of my dad's. This was not a glamorous camping trip; rather, it was more of a "sleep on cots in a green Army tent with two other smelly men" sort of experience. And in all seriousness, it was *fantastic*. Over the four days we were there, it rained, hailed, and snowed, each in near biblical proportions. One night it rained so hard that instead of sleeping we were relegated to taking turns holding the tent flaps shut, lest the deluge overwhelm us and carry us away. All we could do was laugh. That, and shiver, all night long.

This all would have been worth it, if we'd actually bagged a few elk, or even one! But that year it wasn't meant to be. The only thing we caught that week was a head cold, but the trip will live on in my memory for years. Here's the reason why: each morning we'd start the day by reading a few verses from the Bible and then talking about what those Scriptures meant to us. One morning, my dad flipped open his Bible to Psalm 69:6 and read these words: "May those who hope in you not be disgraced because of me, O

Lord, the LORD Almighty; may those who seek you not be put to shame because of me, O God of Israel."

He closed his Bible and looked at us with sincere eyes. "This has been my prayer since the very beginning," he said, "that nothing I *ever* do or say would bring an ounce of shame on the Lord."

I posted a brief video of some of my dad's teaching on YouTube around the same time, and a few days later checked back to find a comment had been posted there by some guy named George M. Several people had posted comments about the segment, but George M.'s is the one I recall. He wrote, "James Dobson is a hater. Take his advice at your own peril."

James Dobson is a hater? *My dad* is a hater? The tiny hairs on my neck stood up straight.

YouTube has this neat little function whereby you can post a comment in response to someone else's comment and in effect carry on a dialogue. And so I did. I wrote: "James Dobson has written more than eighty books, he has broadcast nearly eight thousand radio programs, and he has produced three video series totaling a full thirty hours of film. If he is a 'hater,' as you say he is, then there ought to be plenty of fodder to prove the point. Would you mind pointing me to just one example?"

Of course he didn't write back.

Nobody ever writes back.

George M. didn't write back for the same reason every other person doesn't write back: *they would have absolutely nothing to say.* My dad has not been perfect with his words—the Bible says this is actually an impossibility for us all—but he *has* been careful. Thoughtful. Measured. Sure. He has done what I totally failed to do that day when I used my words to wound my sister: he has refused to bring shame on the Lord.

I've often asked my dad about his commitment to wise speech, and he always points to a single encounter. He was at a book-seller's conference in the late 1970s, when his first book was being released, and hoards of people were clamoring for his attention and his autograph. It was his first real "appearance," and he was struck by how attentive everyone was to every word he spoke. After the crowds died down and the book signing was over, my dad began to pack up his things to head home. It was then that God chose to give my dad a piece of advice. "I am prepared to do great things through you," God said to him, "but you first must learn to tame your tongue."

My dad doesn't really remember what he may have said that day that could even remotely fall into the "untamed" category, but the impression he'd gotten was clear. And it was that divine mandate that has guided my dad all these years. It's a mandate that helps me too, which is good; I need more help than you may know.

Case in point: Laura and I were loading up our kids to go somewhere one afternoon, and we were doing that thing parents of young children do where there's a mad flurry of activity every single time the family departs the house—"Do you have the diaper bag? Yes, and did you remember the sippy cups? No, but I'll grab them, and did you get the address where we're going? Yes, yes, go, go, hurry, or else we're going to be *ridiculously* late." It doesn't mat-ter how far in advance you plan and prepare, the final five minutes prior to departure are always stressful, disorganized, and not fun.

It was during this lovely five-minute segment of time that I happened to notice that while my wife had begun to buckle our son into his car seat, she must have become distracted and had not, in fact, finished the job. Instead of simply completing the task for her or mentioning to my son in a nice, sing-song voice that, "Oops! Mommy and Daddy had better get you all strapped in!" I did what I too often tend to do, which is to let my tongue go totally untamed.

"Uh, Laura?" I said with wide eyes and accusation. "Do you think you might want to actually *buckle* our son into his seat?"

Despite the flurry of activity that had so recently surrounded us, there was now uncomfortable radio silence.

She looked at me. I looked at her. In that moment, we both knew the score.

"Laura," I said, realization settling in. "I am *so sorry* I said it that way. I shouldn't have used that tone with you. I was wrong. Please forgive me?"

See why we pay our marriage counselor the big bucks? This stuff takes training, my friend.

The reality is this: I meant every word of that apology. The last person on the planet I want to wound is my wife. I love my wife. I enjoy my wife. I like making her feel happy instead of miserable and beat down.

As is customary for Laura's nature, she forgave me on the spot and never brought up the incident again. But I bring it up. In my mind and heart, I bring it up. I do it because it reminds me that it takes *hard work* to tame the tongue. The Bible puts it this way: Think about how even the most vicious wildfire was started by a single spark (see James 3:5). That single spark? It's the *tongue*.

Sure, sometimes we use it to praise God, but we can also curse those we say we love. The challenge, then, is this: Either we learn to restrain our tongue's natural inclinations, or else we set fire to our relational world. Unlike his renegade son, my father has always been an absolute *master* of restraint.

James Dobson Jr. rarely did anything in life without first seeking input from James Dobson Sr. My dad is an only child, and when he was growing up, his father was equal parts traveling evangelist and, as I've mentioned, professional artist. The roles took him away from home quite a bit, which only made my dad's time with him more precious. When they were together, they were *together,* and that wonderful intimacy never faded over time.

After my dad grew up and got an education and decided to begin a ministry to serve the family, he called his father to ask whether he should pursue radio or television. He figured these were the means by which he'd reach the most people, but he couldn't decide which approach would be better. "I say go into radio," my grandfather told him, after sitting with the decision awhile. "Radio is more intimate," he explained. "It will be easier to connect with your audience's heart."

That's all my dad needed to hear. And connect with his audience he did, eventually to the tune of three hundred million listeners per week. There was a long stretch in my dad's ministry when his program was the most played radio program on earth; twenty-four hours a day, seven days a week, somewhere in the world it was airing. Somewhere, *somebody* was listening to his show.

My dad tells me now that it was humbling to be invited into people's lives like that. "You rarely listen to radio in a group," he would say. "You listen alone. Whenever I've been on air, I like to think it's just the listener and me, sitting together, having a chat." My dad's respect for the individual coupled with his sense of reverence regarding his role forged in him a deep commitment to using his words wisely, to making every syllable count. He knew from the beginning that words have power, and he was determined to use that power for good.

So, yes, he practiced a certain restraint I seem to have lacked most of my life. But there was something else at work here. He had a goal in mind each time that he spoke—to connect, to unite, to *relate*. Professionally speaking, nothing ever has been more important to my dad than to maintain the trust of his listener, to honor the intimacy he'd built with her or him. For as long as I can remember, he has been studying the art of using words wisely to get better at his vocational craft.

When I was thirteen or fourteen years old, I'd come home from skateboarding with my buddies and often find my dad holed away in his den, his ear inclined toward his stereo, listening to records and tapes. It's probably why I have such an extensive collection of vinyl today; something about those old LPs feels and sounds a lot like home. He'd be listening to Bill Cosby's classic album *Himself,* or to Tony Campolo's *It's Friday, but Sunday's Comin'!* or to any of a dozen other preachers and comedians, and then he'd draw my attention their way. "You hear that, Ryan?" he'd say, all smiles. "Notice how he gives space there for the audience to laugh. *That's* the sign of a master. It doesn't *get* any better than that."

Before I knew it, my dad would be six minutes into a full-on speech about intonation and rhythm, about using humor to let people off the hook. "You can't beat people up all the time, you know?" he'd say. "You have to give them a break every now and then."

Dad would play his favorite talks by his favorite speakers— their "sugar sticks," as he called them—and let himself be schooled by their style and approach. He'd pay attention to how having a dynamite opener would guarantee them five or six subsequent minutes of their audience's rapt attention, and how having a good full minute after that would buy them five or six minutes more. And then he'd set about to craft his own "good minutes," something that would invite his listeners in.

I caught a documentary by Jerry Seinfeld not long ago, in which he throws away all his old material and forces himself to write a new comedy routine from scratch. People think stand-ups have an easy job, that it is somehow *natural* to stand on a stage, grab a mic, and command a crowd for upward of two hours' time. In fact, the opposite is true. The film trails Seinfeld as he bombs time and time again and in some of the very same New York comedy clubs where he originally got his start. "For the normal person," he says, "this is like going to work in your underwear. Imagine showing up at your job tomorrow, with nothing but your skivvies on. This is what it's like to trot out new material. Humbling, every time."

You watch as Seinfeld pulls together a good minute. Then a good five minutes. Then a good ten minutes, then twenty, then more. You *celebrate* with him as he finalizes an entire show— ninety minutes of great, great stuff. And you come away realizing that it's crazy-tough work crafting words that people will care about, words that they'll turn attention to and let seep in.

There's a powerful scene in the book of Matthew, where Jesus is talking to some teachers of the Law. These are learned men, wise men, men who prized religion and the Scriptures and keeping the rules and tattling on those who didn't. Jesus is warning them about quenching the Spirit of God—that is, being so focused on keeping the *rules* of God that you totally neglect *relationship with God*—when He makes this statement: "But I tell you that men will have to give account on the day of judgment for every careless word they have spoken" (Matt. 12:36).

It must have been a sobering thing for those guys to hear. I know it's sobering for me to hear now. Will I really have to stand before God someday and be asked to explain away all my verbal grenades and gaffes? If indeed there's time in heaven, this might take far longer than God expects.

Jesus goes on: "For by your words you will be acquitted, and by your words you will be condemned" (v. 37).

See, this is why words matter—because remember, our words are *who we are*. What Jesus was saying was the same thing Seinfeld was experiencing, which is the same thing my dad always knew to be true: "The power of life and the power of death? That power resides within our words."

I've been making an observation here lately, which is that as a nation our words are tearing us apart. It's impossible to turn on cable news these days without hearing a shouting match erupt. Producers are actually vying for the fight, slating hot-headed pundits from opposing sides for the same panel on the very same night. I come away from watching this stuff with the same thought every time: *We're probably far more united as a country than we know. But we'll never be allowed to link arms.*

Why is this, you ask? Because unity doesn't make for good TV. Blue state/red state, conservative/liberal, us-versus-them—*this* is how ratings soar. But it's also how our souls slowly die.

At a ministry here in town I teach a class I lovingly title, "How to Be a Christian Conservative and Not Be a Jerk." My main premise for that class is that most people—conservative Christians among them—do not know the difference between a conversation and a debate. Indulge me for a moment, if you will.

For the past twenty years, there has been an annual competition in the sports world known as the Ultimate Fighting Championship. Competitors from every major martial-arts discipline—kickboxing, karate, sumo, boxing, savate, taekwondo, jiu jitsu, and shoot fighting—compete in a (mostly) no-holds-barred tournament to determine who is the "ultimate fighting champion" in the end. My wife is repulsed by the fact that I've seen every single fight that has ever been fought, but thankfully, she still sticks by my side.

I've noticed something along the way, as I've been watching all these UFC bouts. When two fighters get into the cage—yes, they fight in a cage . . . *gasp!*—and one fighter throws a punch at the other, the guy who gets clocked very rarely steps back and says, "Hey! He *hit* me, ref!"

He doesn't whine about the punch or pout about the punch or reflect on why the punch came his way. No, no, he *expects* the punch and *receives* the punch because he's a professionally trained athlete who in fact *signed up for a fight.*

Let's port this idea over to the Christian Conservative world for a moment, shall we? A Christian Conservative posts something on Facebook and soon after discovers a non-Christian, non-Conservative has said something contrary in response. The Christian Conservative then launches an all-out war, declaring the non-Christian, non-Conservative irresponsible and malicious and proof that all those conspiracies really do exist.

The non-Christian, non-Conservative steps away thinking, *Touchy, touchy, touchy! I was just having a little fun.* But it's much too late now, I think you'd agree. The horse has already left the barn.

There is a vast difference between a conversation and a debate. A debate is a *fight*, and you can't take on someone who hasn't signed up for a fight.

Here's how the Bible puts it: You who say you love God? *You* be the ones to seek peace.

When things escalate, *you* bring them down a notch.

When temperatures rise, *you* cool things off.

When opinions are flying, *you* work to find common ground.

When fists clench, *you* speak loving words.

Of course there is a time for debate here and there; I happen to *love* dismantling other people's views. But you'd better believe I make sure the "other" in that equation is ready to take me on. Because nine times out of ten what the "other" is looking for is a friendly chat, not a fiery debate.

I trained for a while with a mixed-martial-arts coach, and he gave me the very same advice my debate coach in high school had given me years before. "When you take someone on," they both said, "you don't want to beat them so badly that they never want to face you again. You want to beat them so badly that they never want to face *anyone* again. You want them to face you and then absolutely give up the fight."

The apostle Paul says that we should always be prepared to give a reason for the hope that lies within us, but I have to tell you from personal experience, this almost never involves a fight. Sure, there has been the rare occasion when I have *debated* someone into the kingdom—they agreed to the fight, they took me on, and they came away with white flag raised. But 99.9 percent of the time it doesn't happen this way; mostly it happens by way of a *chat*. A conversation. A dialogue. A free and friendly exchange of ideas. It happens when I choose to listen well and love well and leave the cage fighting to the pros.

My father's genius in this regard has always been his ability to calmly and logically explain what he believes, and then to explain why he believes it. Both are critically important. Let's say a colleague of yours from work knows your beliefs and asks you one day, "Why is it so wrong for me to sleep with my girlfriend before marriage? I mean, *I love her.* Isn't that what counts?" Too many lovers of God miss a great opportunity for healthy dialogue here by tossing out grenades instead. "Premarital sex is a *sin!*" they rant. "And sin can land you in a little place called *hell!*" Or they'll say, "You don't *really* love her, if you're willing to totally lead her astray." Or this one, which is my personal favorite: "The Bible says it. I believe it. End of story."

Talk about a quick way to end a conversation before it ever gets off the ground.

My dad was posed this type of question thousands of times in front of my adolescent watchful eye, and each time, I watched him solicit dialogue rather than squelch it. It was a beautiful thing.

"Well," he'd say, in a situation like this one I'm describing, "here's my thinking. All of life seems to point to a divine Creator, to God. The natural world, our own anatomy, the whole idea of the family, and so forth—based on what I understand about this world in which we live, *everything* points to Him. And if *that's* true, then our finances point to Him, and physics points to Him, and archaeology points to Him, and art points to Him, and our relationships point to Him, including my relationship with my wife, and including your relationship with your girlfriend. Based on this, the question in my mind would be, *how* is that relationship pointing to God? How is sleeping with your girlfriend pointing to God?"

He'd then pause. And lean in. And listen with thoughtful attention as the guy rattled off his own worldview. Then my dad would ask a few questions; then the other man would ask a few questions—they'd go back and forth in conversation, not debating, not splitting hairs, and not getting angry or judgmental or cold. Just talking. Listening. Freely exchanging heartfelt ideals. The lesson I've taken away from observing countless situations such as this one is that when you learn to convey your deepest beliefs in a way that is engaging and entertaining, restrained and yet funny, humble and also provocative, logical and well thought out, you can't *imagine* how powerful your words can be.

And the best news of all? We can start using words well today. We can say, "I love you." We can say, "I'm sorry." We can say, "I had no business mouthing off." We can say any of a thousand honest sentiments, all aimed at encouraging, connecting, building up. The power of life, and the power of death, right? That power resides in our words.

finding your exceptional life

1. Describe an experience where you realized with fresh awareness the power of your words.

2. What do you think of the idea that our words—simple syllables we choose to speak—can actually bring shame on the Lord?

3. What words do you wish you had the courage to speak, and to whom do you wish you could speak them? Consider speaking them now to God, and then ask Him to provide an open door for you to say what needs to be said.

16

believe

Every man must do two things alone;
he must do his own believing and his own dying.
—Martin Luther

I prayed a prayer to "give my heart to Jesus" when I was three years old, but it would take me twenty-seven more years to begin to appreciate the gravity of the decision I'd made. Yes, biblical-worldview summer camp back at age seventeen had filled my mind with all manner of sound ideas, but until those ideas were forced to stand up against real-life travails, I wouldn't know which of them I truly believed. Someone once said, "Faith isn't faith until it's all you're holding onto." Age thirty is when I'd prove that quote true.

One afternoon during that bleak and despairing year, my buddy Lindsey called, and partway through what I thought was a benign conversation, he paused and then asked, "Hey, man, are you mad at me? You seem a little . . . I don't know . . ."

His question caught me off guard. "Huh? Of course not!" I said. "Why would I be mad at you?"

"Are you okay?" he then asked, a question whose only answer was no. I told Lindsey my wife was leaving me and that I wasn't really sure what to do. He registered his shock and then said, "Listen, you need to come surfing. It will be good for you to hang out with the guys, and being outside can't hurt, either."

"The guys" Lindsey was referring to were a tight group of eight or nine men who surfed together a couple of times a week. They loved Jesus, they were loyal to each other, and they'd tried to rope me into their posse on several occasions before.

"I don't know . . ." I began, just as Lindsey was saying, "I won't tell them anything about what you're going through. Just come, Ryan. It will do you worlds of good."

I lost count of how many times Lindsey invited me surfing before I finally accepted his offer, but eventually I did go. He was elated I'd said yes and told me where to be and when. "We leave my house at five," I heard him say, just before I heard myself say, "A.M.?"

To be at his house by five a.m., I'd have to leave my apartment by four. Which was a problem for me because I already had plans at four, plans to be passed out in my bed. For months on end, I had been sleeping sixteen hours a day, leaving my bedroom only to go to the bathroom, get something to drink, or replenish my junk-food supply. I was subsisting in a state of massive depression and would wind up becoming literally a glimmer of myself before that season was said and done; I went from one hundred and

eighty pounds to a buck thirty-five, which bore out the fact that
if you need an effective diet plan, just introduce a little stress into
your life.

"Yeah, man!" Lindsey was saying. "Five o'clock in the *a.m.,*
bro! You'll love it. Nothing like beating the sun to the beach. So,
we're good, right? See you then?"

Sure, Lindsey. Whatever you say.

I wasn't with "the guys" five minutes before I knew I shouldn't
have come. They were all morning people who were more chipper
at five a.m. than I was at *any* point in the day. What's more, the
wetsuit they'd loaned me was way too big, which meant the icy
water of the Pacific flowed right through it, keeping me perpetually chilled to the bone. But moments later, I'd be handed fresh
perspective, courtesy of God Himself.

We all started paddling out, and as the first burst of cold water
washed over me, I had that sensation you get when you've swum
down a little too deep in the ocean and upon resurfacing inhale
a huge breath of long-awaited air. The wave flowed over my head
and down my back and off my toes, and with it took every ounce
of stress I'd been carrying for the better part of a full calendar
year. For the first time in a long time, I could breathe. I mean
really breathe—deep, meaningful, diaphragm-expanding breaths.
Chains that had restricted my chest for way too long were somehow miraculously loosed.

I straddled my long board and reflexively began testing my
breath. Thankfully none of the guys were right next to me; if any
of them had seen what I was doing, they would have thought I was
at best a kook. I inhaled four counts and then exhaled four counts

and then did it all over again. I could breathe. *I could breathe.* What on earth was going on?

Evidently a decent wave was headed my way, because I start hearing the guys hollering, "Go for it, Ryan! It's all you!" Surfing is no easy sport, but I was committed to the wave, and I rode it nearly one hundred yards to the wild screams and cheers of eight men still on the water before I eased my board ashore. And I laughed the whole way in.

The axis on which my entire world spun changed on that September day in San Clemente. Perhaps for the first time in my life, my faith was real, and it was mine. "Trust Me," I kept sensing God saying that day. "I'm going to take care of you."

The vastness of the ocean was all the proof I needed that my circumstances, while in my view overwhelming, were not too big for Him.

Lindsey was right all along. I did wind up loving those five a.m. excursions, and within no time, I'd make surfing a daily part of my life. The ocean was my sanctuary, and God was faithful to meet with me there. Slowly—*very* slowly—but surely, He'd start to put me back together again.

Not long after that initial trip with Lindsey, I was scheduled to see my mom and dad. It had been a while since we'd been together, which was 100 percent my fault. I was James Dobson's son and I couldn't keep my marriage together. You see the tension here.

But my father never once played that card; instead, he simply went to the place of concern. I was always a happy, gregarious kid, and yet now I was an emaciated insomniac on a veritable menu of very strong meds keeping me from driving off a bridge or punching someone in the face. He took one look at me and began then and there a campaign to get me to camp.

Mention "camp" in the Dobson household, and the conversation will undoubtedly wind up at Joe White's feet. Since the early 1970s, Joe White has owned and served as president of Missouri-based Kanakuk Kamps and for decades has been, according to my dad, the foremost authority on teenagers in this country. Joe is something of a miracle worker when it comes to kids; when it comes to cracking cynical shells, tearing down fortified walls, and restoring long-since lost hope, he is *legend*. In short, my dad wanted me to go to camp.

"Dad, I'm *thirty*," I clarified. "Thirty-year-olds don't go to camp."

Which is when I began receiving calls on my cell phone from none other than Joe himself. "Come hang out with us for a month," he'd say, in his classically easy-going style. Joe has white hair, a year-long tan, and looks like someone who would be working as a featured ukulele player for the Beach Boys. He's approachable. He's kind. He's chill. I didn't stand a chance.

What I couldn't possibly know as I boarded the plane for Branson was that my already terrible set of life circumstances was about to get even worse. Lawyers were calling me and leaving angry messages, threatening to take every last penny I owned— they actually did take all of those pennies, as well as a bunch I *didn't* own—and going in debt on par with that can really drag a good man down. But each day at camp, I'd wake up, and I'd head to the dining hall. And there, I'd feed myself the first real food I'd eaten in a long time.

I'd slowly put back on some needed weight, which made my energy level rise. I'd reconnect with God in ways I didn't know I could. And I'd reflect on the darkest season of my life as one who was finally seeing some light.

Nearly every day at Kanakuk found me sunning on the boat dock alone. I'd wait until campers' activities were through and then settle myself onto an abandoned surfboard and paddle myself around the lake. It was there I did most of my thinking—about where I'd been and who I was now. One afternoon I had a wild flashback that took me all the way back to age seventeen. I was sitting in class at the worldview camp and heard a lecture from a man who could recite poetry as though reading verses from the back of his hand. He had inspired me to begin reading poetry back then, and Kipling was a favorite of mine. I'd read his *Gods of the Copybook Headings* upward of one hundred times, a poem that never failed to choke me up. The poem is about truth, and how it has an uncanny way of always being true.

The "copybooks" of old were paper-bound books with statements reflecting the essence of human wisdom at the top of each page and a full spread of horizontal lines below, on which schoolchildren learning their alphabet would write and write and write. They'd copy those headings in order to learn the curls of p's and q's, but in the process, that wisdom would get in them somehow. Repetition has a way of cementing ideas, and so little kids were unwittingly made wise.

In the poem, Rudyard Kipling presents a series of economic affronts to truth but notes that in the end, truth still prevails. It begins:

As it will be in the future, it was at the birth of Man—

There are only four things certain since Social Progress began—

That the Dog returns to his Vomit and the Sow returns to her Mire,

And the burnt Fool's bandaged finger goes wabbling back to the Fire—

And that after this is accomplished, and brave new world begins

When all men are paid for existing and no man must pay for his sins

As surely as Water will wet us, as surely as Fire will burn

The Gods of the Copybook Headings with terror and slaughter return.

The Gods of the Copybook Headings—truth itself—will always return. Truth can't help but remain true. And while my woes were far more widespread than economic—they included declines on spiritual, physical, relational, and emotional fronts as well—the point stuck. Truth was still truth, and in terms of the multifaceted bondage I felt back then, it would be simple truths that would set me free.

Five years ago I was at my parents' house, rummaging through one of the storage closets in their basement, looking for a movie to watch. I fingered the spines of a dozen or so DVDs before I landed on a rubber-banded package of jewel cases that had a handwritten piece of paper attached to the front. "Focus on the Family, Film Series 1," it read. My dad's first film series was recorded in 1978. Seeing my dad in the 70s? Now *that* was quality entertainment. I stuffed the batch in my bag and decided to take it home so that Laura and I could watch it together.

Later that evening, she and I parked ourselves on the couch in our living room and aired that very first film. My dad took the stage before a live audience, and immediately my wife and I poked fun. The full sideburns! The giant eyeglasses! The way-too-wide lapels! We had a lot of laughs at my dad's expense. And then we heard my dad speak.

Within five minutes, we both were in tears.

He was speaking of fatherhood in that talk, and specifically about the epidemic among fathers he referred to as "if-then" parenting. "*If* I can just get past this deadline, *then* I'll spend more time with the kids." "*If* I can just get through this busy season, *then* I'll make little Joey's baseball games." "*If* I can just close this deal, *then* I'll take some time off."

But even when those "ifs" do happen, the marker simply gets moved. Now there's another "if" that's pointed to, as the time when Daddy finally acts like a dad. There's always one more thing to do that seems more important than fathering a child.

I sat there beside my wife, both of us staring at an ancient visage of my dad on screen, and I knew that from that moment forward, I would be a better dad. I would be a better husband. I shook my head slowly as I watched that man in the obnoxious three-piece suit with six-inch-wide tie move across the stage, calmly and confidently delivering his content, thinking, *He's been my truth-teller my entire life.* His perspectives on life and on love, on faith and on family, on godliness and goodness and more, had been the copybook headings I'd unknowingly absorbed, for almost four decades' time.

It had been eight years since my divorce by that point, and so much had occurred in my life. The day my ex-wife told me she was leaving, I remember thinking, *That's it for me. I'm done.* I'd been in ministry to that point, and I *loved* it. But who wanted to be ministered to by a guy whose world was falling apart?

I went to bed that night thinking I'd probably have to get a job in IT, or go back into the construction business, seeing as aside from ministry, those were the only two things I could do. Maybe that wouldn't be so bad; after all, it's kind of fun to build stuff—computers, houses, whatever. It's just that "building stuff" isn't what fired me up in the mornings; teaching people about God is what did. I saw myself as a gourmet chef who'd been kicked out of the kitchen and told he could never cook again. My heart had been broken. My faith had been rocked. My *everything* was reduced to shreds.

And yet it was during those bleakest of bleak days that I found an intimacy with God I'd not known.

During my stay at Kanakuk, a short guy who drove a big truck came up to me one day at the dock and said, "Ryan, God gave me a verse to give to you."

I was skeptical at first; if God wanted me to have a verse, why couldn't He give it to me Himself?

But then I considered the messenger. This particular person was known primarily for keeping his open Bible perched on his steering wheel while driving around town, so that he could consume God's Word during his daily comings and goings. So while I might have questioned his driving safety, I didn't question his spiritual depth.

The verse was James 2:23, which reads, "And the scripture was fulfilled that says, 'Abraham believed God, and it was credited to him as righteousness,' and he was called God's friend."

I desperately needed those words. I needed to be told, "Believe God! And things will go well for you." In the end that's exactly what I chose to do. I chose to simply believe God.

Recently I watched an interview with a well-known actor who was describing some tough times he walked through as a teenager and early twenty-something. He was raised by Christian parents and had three siblings who also followed Christ, but he got to a point in his life when he questioned whether the "faith thing" was real. By his own admission, he started hanging out with friends who didn't have his best interest at heart; and before he knew it he had a full-blown addiction to alcohol and drugs.

He said he woke up one morning in the cab of his pickup truck and had no idea where he was. He looked around and saw proof that he'd been in an accident—his truck was stuck in a ditch, his driver-side door was open and beat up, and he himself had bloody scrapes and bruises all over his face and arms. "I must have been stoned and then decided to drive," he said. "I hope I didn't run over anyone during that trip."

The truth is, he doesn't know what he did during that hazy, influenced drive.

One of his brothers finally figured out what was going on and approached him one afternoon. "I know what you've been up to," the brother said, "and we want to have a little talk."

The "we" here was the entire family, who had gathered to intervene.

As this guy made his way into his parents' living room, he noticed his father and brothers seated there. They confronted him about his behavior and gave him two options from which to choose: "You either can go God's way with your life," the father said, "or you can leave this family and try to make it on your own."

There it was, the line in the sand. Which way would he go?

He told the interviewer that immediately his heart was contrite. "I fell to my knees at my father's feet," he said, "and I cried like a baby that day. I knew I deserved to be kicked out of the family, but here were the people I love most in the world telling me I could come back home if I wanted to."

After he composed himself enough to choke out a few words, he looked into his father's eyes and said, "What took you so long?"

What took you so long?

On the heels of long-awaited rescue, we tend to ask God the very same thing. We finally get a glimpse of the street signs pointing us toward home and look heavenward with incredulity written all over our face. *What took you so long?* we wonder, to which our loving Father says, "I was here all along."

That's the truth, you know, and truth can't help but stay true. God is always at home—ready to receive us, ready to help. It is we who have gone for a walk.

finding your exceptional life

1. What has your "belief journey" looked like so far?

2. Where do you still struggle to fully trust God?

3. What questions do you want God to provide answers for, so that you can wholeheartedly believe that He is who He says He is and that He will do all He says He will do?

This book is dedicated to my
hero, role model, friend, and father
James Dobson.
I love you.

acknowledgments

To **Laura** my sweet wife, for putting up with my neuroses while the writing process bogged down. For being an amazing wife and mother. I love you so much. What an adventure we have together. I'd do it all over again a thousand times (of course this is all about you).

To **Lincoln Cash** and **Luci Rose** for being the inspiration for this book. For making me want to be a better dad to you both! I love you MORE!!

To **Robert Wolgemuth** for talking me into this project and then talking me down when the first publishers didn't bite. For all the support, love, and encouragement, and for knowing exactly what I need to hear and when. For believing in me when I didn't. For working with the whole Dobson clan on "Legacy" with grace and joy. To your sweet wife **Bobbie** for letting you travel and work too hard through all the good times and trials. I love you too. I can't believe we've known each other for almost thirty-five years. I hope we have thirty-five more!

To **Ashley Wiersma** for rescuing me as I stared down death's door and for accepting this project in the midst of taking care of your own family. For finding my voice and helping me *really* tell my story. I absolutely could NOT have done this without you. You will always be my first choice for future projects. I hope we get to share many many more!

Thanks to **Perry** and **Prisca** for putting up with endless e-mails, texts, and phone calls interrupting family time.

To **Matt McCartie** for giving me the courage to stand up in front of a bunch of strangers so long ago. That trip to Hume set me on my course. And for always being creative and artistic and for wearing your heart on your sleeve. It was and is a great example.

To **Doug Boemler Wareing** for all the bios, bumpers, tags, and talks. Thanks for putting super complex life struggles into very simple words. I'll always picture you in a green Cadillac with gold, wire rims. A classic! Love to Laura and the kids too! They always make me feel welcome no matter how late it is.

To **Tim Ferriss** for being an inspiration and for showing me new ways to work, live, and cook!

To **Sid Stankovitz** for being a good friend. For paying dues and for giving a bunch of lost kids a place and purpose. And, of course, for all the art. I still have a little room left.

To **everyone** I've left out, and I'm sure there are plenty. Don't take it too hard. If you know me well, then you understand.

And last, but not least, to the **SOC** thank you for wasting countless hours of my time on pointless arguments. I hate you all. Especially your drums..

notes

1. Ryan Dobson, *2Die4: The Dangerous Truth about Following Christ* (New York: Multnomah, 2004), 17–18.

2. James Dobson, *The New Dare to Discipline: The Bestselling Classic for a New Generation of Parents and Teachers* (Carol Stream, IL: Tyndale, 1992), 75.

3. James Dobson, *Love Must Be Tough: New Hope for Marriages in Crisis* (Sisters, OR: Multnomah, 1983), 224–26.

4. Kay Hymowitz, *Ready or Not: What Happens When We Treat Children as Small Adults* (San Francisco: Encounter Books, 2000), 2.

5. Timothy Ferriss, *The 4-Hour Chef: The Simple Path to Cooking Like a Pro, Learning Anything, and Living the Good Life* (New York: Melcher Media, 2012), 23.

6. For the commission's complete report, visit http://www.porn-report.com/attorney-generals-commission-pornography.htm.

7. See http://www.porn-report.com/attorney-generals-commission-pornography.htm; retrieved 12 December 2013.

8 See http://govinfo.library.unt.edu/ngisc/reports/fullrpt.html; retrieved 12 December 2013.

9. See http://www.propertyrightsresearch.org/articles5/dobson_speaks_out_about_terri_sc.htm; retrieved 12 December 2013.

10. See http://wernerbiblecommentary.org/?q=book/print/280.

11. Malcolm Gladwell, *David and Goliath: Underdogs, Misfits, and the Art of Battling Giants* (New York: Little, Brown and Company, 2013), 13.